Praise for

"An innovative take on mastering the
solutions that leaders and employees ne
it and so will you after you read this boo...
Jon Acuff, *New York Times* bestsell...
the Surprising Solution to Overthinking

"Kristel Bauer inspires people to wake up, get off autopilot, and make the positive changes we
need for more happiness and success."
Jason Feifer, editor in chief, *Entrepreneur* magazine

"Kristel's take on mastering leadership in the modern world provides a fresh and needed
perspective for all organizations. With so many approachable strategies to increase happiness,
enhance well-being and optimize performance, *Work-Life Tango* is a must read for anyone looking
to thrive in their personal and professional life!"
Susan MacKenty Brady, *Wall Street Journal* bestselling author of *Arrive & Thrive*;
CEO, Simmons University Institute for Inclusive Leadership

"A must-read for anyone looking for more fulfillment in their work and life! *Work-Life Tango*
gives you permission to stop striving for the old model of work/life balance that breeds
perfectionism and guilt, allowing you to find more deep-rooted happiness, fun and success in
all areas of your life."
Alexandra Carter, Professor, Columbia Law School & *Wall Street Journal*
bestselling author of *Ask for More*

"In today's chaotic world, being a better version of ourselves is challenging. After reading
Work-Life Tango, I now have a fresh perspective, with applicable tools to help shift my thinking
and behaviors to find harmony, happiness and peace with self, others, and the world."
Christine Farrell, CEO of Washington Speakers Bureau

"As the Founder of Hedley and Bennett, I know the challenges that pop up while raising babies
and running a business, while also trying to be on top of your personal life and self-care routine.
Add in remote and hybrid work and things can get even more crazy! There is a serious need
for a roadmap to offer support in these areas and Kristel does an incredible job providing this
in *Work-Life Tango*. A must-read for all leaders and individuals trying to have more happiness
and success in their work and life!"
Ellen Marie Bennett, Founder of Hedley & Bennett,
author of *Dream First, Details Later*

"Stress happens when we focus too much on our own success at work. Kristel Bauer gives us
all permission to let go and embrace a healthier balance, one where purpose and intentionality
reign supreme."
John Brandon, *Forbes* columnist

"*Work-Life Tango* is a refreshing and insightful guide that delves into the complexities of balancing
work and life in the modern world. Kristel Bauer's comprehensive and practical approach to
achieving a fulfilling work-life balance has transformed how I balance my professional and personal
life. Her engaging metaphors and actionable strategies make it a must-read for anyone looking to
thrive in the modern workplace while maintaining a joyful and meaningful personal life."
Angela Schelp, Founder & Co-Owner of Executive Speakers Bureau

"After years of working in the mental health sector, speaking with countless experts and practicing
what she preaches, Kristel Bauer seems to have cracked the elusive code on the perpetual struggle
between a successful career and a fulfilling life. It comes as no surprise that the answer begins with
an honest, at times uncomfortable, internal evaluation. But with her relevant, practical advice
and clear guide to making small, integral adjustments, Kristel confirms that doing the Work-
Life Tango is attainable and sustainable, at a time when we all have been conditioned to believe
otherwise. Her book gives me hope and a road map to more joyful living!"
Gail Simmons, Food Expert, TV Host and author of *Bringing It Home*

"Having 8 kids and multiple businesses plus a tv show can make it really hard to find a work-life balance! I love the advice and practical application that Kristel shares in her book and you should definitely check it out."

Luke Caldwell, HGTV Star Boise Boys; Founder of Timber and Love

"*Work-Life Tango* deeply resonated with me as an entrepreneur who had to navigate the complexities of transitioning a global business to a remote and hybrid work environment during and after COVID. The challenges were immense—balancing productivity, maintaining team morale, and managing my own well-being in an unprecedented time. Bauer's approach to "work-life harmony" rather than "work-life balance" truly struck a chord. She offers not just theory, but practical strategies and personal anecdotes that feel incredibly relevant. Her book is a guide for anyone striving to create a meaningful and fulfilling life, where professional success and personal happiness can coexist, even in the most challenging circumstances. For anyone looking to find their rhythm in the new world of work, *Work-Life Tango* is an essential read."

Daniel Hodgdon, Founder of Vegamour

"Whilst the challenges of hybrid work have been well-documented, there are very few sources that offer useful remedies. Kristel Bauer's thought-provoking work does exactly that, getting beyond the bumper-sticker slogans to offer a myriad of practical solutions."

Martin G Moore, *Wall Street Journal* bestselling author, *No Bullsh!t Leadership*

"In a world where personal and work-related stress continues to rise, Kristel offers readers practical advice for navigating and alleviating these pressures. Drawing from her expertise and real-life experience, she shares a wealth of ideas, techniques, and tips that cover every aspect of wellbeing. This book encourages readers to reflect on their own lives and purpose before delving into key topics to develop effective wellbeing strategies. The beauty of *Work-Life Tango* lies in its versatility—you can enjoy it in one sitting or explore individual chapters for actionable insights to enhance your wellbeing both at home and at work."

Andy Hawkes, CEO Cardinus Risk Management

"Performing the tango is all about connection, balance, and authentic improvisation. Drawing on deep research and experience, Kristel Bauer is a skillful teacher of the tango of modern life. Her work is a valuable gift to busy, mission-driven people who want to lead more joy, intention, and presence."

Justin Talbot Zorn; co-author, *Golden: The Power of Silence in a World of Noise*

"If you want to learn how to navigate work and life and optimize health, then *Work-Life Tango* is a must read for success. Kristel Bauer brings you practical steps for achieving happiness, well-being and your personal best while avoiding burn out. Now, more than ever, her holistic approach will change your life and outlook for the future. If you are want to bring forth your best, learn how to do the Work-Life Tango."

William W. Li, MD, *New York Times* bestselling author of *Eat to Beat Disease* and *Eat to Beat Your Diet*

"The constant pursuit of work-life balance can take a toll on our physical and mental health if not managed properly. This book is the perfect guide for high achievers, with a refreshing perspective to become unstoppable through actionable strategies to thrive in the hybrid work landscape we live in today."

Alden Mills, Inc. 500 CEO, Entrepreneur, bestselling author, former Navy SEAL

Work-Life Tango

Finding Happiness, Harmony and
Peak Performance Wherever You Work

Kristel Bauer

First published by John Murray Business in 2024
An imprint of John Murray Press

1

Copyright © Kristel Bauer 2024

The right of Kristel Bauer to be identified as the Author of the Work has been asserted by her in
accordance with the Copyright, Designs and Patents Act 1988.

All rights reserved. No part of this publication may be reproduced, stored in a retrieval system, or
transmitted, in any form or by any means without the prior written permission of the publisher,
nor be otherwise circulated in any form of binding or cover other than that in which it is published
and without a similar condition being imposed on the subsequent purchaser.

This book is for information or educational purposes only and is not intended to act as a substitute
for medical advice or treatment. Any person with a condition requiring medical attention should
consult a qualified medical practitioner or suitable therapist.

A CIP catalogue record for this title is available from the British Library

Trade Paperback ISBN 978 1 39981 7 455
UK ebook ISBN 978 1 39981 7 462

Typeset by KnowledgeWorks Global Ltd.

Printed and bound in the United States of America

John Murray Press policy is to use papers that are natural, renewable and recyclable products
and made from wood grown in sustainable forests. The logging and manufacturing processes
are expected to conform to the environmental regulations of the country of origin.

John Murray Press
Carmelite House
50 Victoria Embankment
London EC4Y 0DZ

John Murray Business
123 S. Broad St., Ste 2750
Philadelphia, PA 19109

www. johnmurraypress.co.uk

The authorised representative in the EEA is Hachette Ireland, 8 Castlecourt Centre,
Castleknock Road, Castleknock, Dublin 15, D15 YF6A, Ireland

John Murray Press, part of Hodder & Stoughton Limited
An Hachette UK company

Contents

CONTENTS

Foreword

Modern humans strive for work-life balance as if it's a binary choice. Constantly maintaining the perfect equilibrium between work and life is illusive for a reason—it's not possible. Extraordinary achievements require times of extraordinary effort when personal compromises are made in order to achieve the audacious goal. These times when we run hot must then be interspersed with hours or days of recovery. I call these periods of adult play 'productive unproductivity'. The work-life balance comes not in the dogmatic adherence to a scripted schedule, but in the awareness of the baseline, and returning to it at regular intervals to re-evaluate, recharge and recommit to our dreams.

Joy in life comes from being intentional in everything we do, including facing our fears. In my experience as the co-founder and CEO of RSE Ventures, a guest Shark on ABC's Shark Tank, the author of *Burn the Boats*, and as an Executive Fellow at Harvard Business School, I have seen the most ambitious individuals fall short for the same reason: they never confront the metaphorical boats—the backup plans and lingering insecurities—that summon us to retreat from our own potential.

In the pursuit of our life's greatest purpose, it's tempting to fall in the trap of focusing on the future and forfeiting the present. To truly transcend and achieve our true potential, we need to completely replace our model of work/life balance with one that actually fits with the modern world. No longer are we able to fit work, relationships, and personal fulfillment into tidy little boxes. In our current age of remote work, endless scrolling on social media, and constantly evolving relationship advice, it can feel like you're "always on". Kristel's book offers a healthier and integrative approach to building a life you don't need to escape from.

When I first met Kristel on her Live Greatly podcast back in 2021, I discovered that we both shared a desire to live life to the fullest and to help others do the same. I was thrilled to learn that Kristel was writing a book to help people thrive at work and in life. As a corporate wellness and performance expert, keynote speaker and the founder of Live Greatly, Kristel brings a unique and eye-opening perspective to finding more happiness and success amid this new world of work. With Kristel's background in healthcare, her experience in Integrative Psychiatry and Integrative Medicine, and her presence in the speaking and media space, she can address the real everyday struggles and pain points that hybrid workers, remote workers, and leadership teams face. This book will reframe the way you balance the ambitious pursuits in both your personal and professional life.

Matt Higgins
Wall Street Journal bestselling author of *Burn the Boats*

The dance of work and life

• • •

Your life is made up of a variety of choices. Some big and some small. But one thing they all have in common is they make an impact. Whether it is how you spend your time or what you have for breakfast, these decisions can put you on a clear path towards fulfillment, on a bumpy road filled with stress, or stuck in one place like a broken-down car without a tow truck in sight. Wherever you are at on your work/life journey, recognize that every moment is an opportunity. An opportunity to respond in a new way, think in a new way, and behave in a new way. An opportunity to move one step closer to who you aspire to be.

The world may have led you to believe that you can't be at the top of your game in your career while also being a great parent, partner, and friend. That you need to put your well-being on the back burner to advance in your career, or that you need to sacrifice things you truly want and need to be successful. I'm here to tell you that these interpretations of successfully navigating work and life are completely mis-guided. While challenges and setbacks are inevitable, you can create a work/life where you incorporate all the components you truly need to be fulfilled. You can fill your days with the things that really matter to you. With the things that light you up and get you jumping out of bed each morning. You can excel in your career, wherever you work, have nourishing relationships, and have a fun life that you absolutely love.

Getting to a place where you are happy with where you are and with where you are going is also good for business. Research shows that happier employees are more productive employees, with one study[1] even showing that happier individuals were about 12% more productive. Data[2] also shows that happier leaders cultivate more engaged teams and happier employees. The bottom line is, when you feel good, everyone benefits.

As a hybrid or remote worker, I'm sure you've heard people talk about the importance of work/life balance, but I'm curious: What pops into your mind when you think of this phrase? Does it leave you feeling empowered or happy? Or does it make you feel stressed or perhaps a bit guilty? For many, the idea of work/life balance seems unattainable, and it doesn't fit the mold of their current reality. Personally, when I hear this phrase, it makes me feel like opposing sides are fighting for my attention. It leaves me with a sense of pressure and guilt, suggesting I need to choose between a career I thoroughly enjoy and a family I dearly love. I'm all for avoiding overworking and delegating appropriate time to the things that matter, but there is a better way to frame it that is more attainable and that won't leave you feeling guilty.

When people talk about wanting work/life balance, I believe what they are really seeking is a *feeling*. An internal feeling of harmony, happiness, meaning, and purpose. Have you ever been fully engrossed in a dance with a partner that you loved, or watched two people dancing where they looked totally in sync? There is a give and take, an ebb and flow, where the partners work together in a seemingly effortless rhythm, resulting in a feeling of freedom and aliveness. Many people are looking for those feelings in their careers and in their lives. They want to have an *inner balance* and the knowledge that they are living meaningful lives. Finding these feelings can be exceptionally difficult though, especially with societal norms constantly telling us that what we do is never enough, in addition to an out-dated model of work/life balance leaving many with feelings of guilt and unhappiness.

Throughout my personal journey, I have learned a new way to view work/life balance that is both empowering and meaningful. By adopting a model of *work/life harmony* I have been able to fill my work and life with all the unique ingredients that matter to me. Just like a dance with great partners who flow together with ease, sometimes work or life may take the lead and the other will need to gracefully adapt. However, if work and life are not in alignment and have different agendas, well . . . things can get awkward, even uncomfortable. Ultimately, they need to work together, supporting each other and complementing one another along the way.

This new work/life model starts with building awareness. Many people get stuck just going through the motions, unintentionally settling for lives and careers that are unfulfilling, consistently being immersed in the mundane. By taking time to get clear on what really matters to you, you will move in the direction of uncovering and expressing your unique personal mission. Once you have clarity on where things are at and what is meaningful to you, it will be time to work on improving your mindset for optimal health, happiness, and success at work and at home. You will discover how to support yourself in breaking free of limiting beliefs, better managing your time, boosting your productivity, and prioritizing the things that truly matter to you by using solution-focused strategies like reframing, mindfulness, time blocking, and active listening. You will learn ways to overcome procrastination and how to optimize your performance as a remote or hybrid worker. You will figure out how to integrate life back into your hybrid or remote workday with micro-self-care breaks, and how to make a healthy lifestyle a natural part of your everyday. You will no longer only have your "life" segmented into "before" and "after" work, as is expected with the work/life balance model, but the parts of your life that light you up will become a part of your entire day, leading to more fun, better relationships, and more happiness. If you are a manager, team leader, or executive, you will discover critical insights to successfully lead remote and hybrid teams while embracing your authentic self.

We are all given checkpoints in our lives. Moments and experiences that help us define who we are and what matters most. These checkpoints are opportunities for us to decide what we want to do with the precious time that we have in this world. They allow us to reflect on where we are and who we want to be. The COVID-19 pandemic was a universal checkpoint for all of humanity. It forced us into our homes to take a close look at our lives, our work, our relationships, and ourselves. There was a surge of remote work and suddenly the barrier between home life and work dissipated and the demands on workers' time and energy doubled, even tripled.

This book is your checkpoint for your current work/life model. It will help you see what is working and what isn't. It will provide you with insights and actionable strategies to get on a path for attaining your version of work/life harmony. Hybrid and remote work are incredible opportunities to answer your inner yearning for more. More happiness, more joy, more meaning, more fun. Not just before or after work, but throughout your entire workday, and throughout your entire life. It's time to start having harmony at work and at home. Your journey starts now.

Endnotes

1 Oswald, A.J., Proto, E., & Srgoi, D. (2015) Happiness and Productivity, *Journal of Labor Economics*, 33(4): 789–822. https://doi.org/10.1086/681096

2 Yan, Y., Zhang, J., Akhtar, M.N., & Liang, S. (2021) Positive leadership and employee engagement: The roles of state positive affect and individualism-collectivism, *Current Psychology*, 42(11): 9109–18. https://doi.org/10.1007/s12144-021-02192-7

PART I

Happy, guilt-free you

CHAPTER 1

When you think you're doing the tango but you're really doing the chicken dance

* * *

Have you ever caught your reflection in a mirror while dancing, or watched a video of yourself at a wedding, and your actual dance moves looked nothing like you were envisioning? Perhaps the movements that you thought looked smooth and on beat actually looked a bit awkward. I have caught snippets of myself dancing in wedding videos, and every time it has resulted in a strong inner pang of awkwardness. While perfecting your dance moves might not be a top priority for you, this same concept applies to all the things that really matter in your work/life. Often, our personal interpretation of what we think we look like, what we think we sound like, or what we think we are doing can differ from the real thing.

I remember when I was rehearsing for my TEDx Talk back in 2021. I decided to start practicing my talk while looking at myself in the mirror and wow, was it uncomfortable at first. I noticed facial expressions that I didn't like, hand movements that seemed excessive, and the reflection that I saw in the mirror wasn't matching up with the image that I had been picturing in my mind. I found myself thinking, do I always slightly smile when I am uncomfortable? Do I really use my hands that much while talking? While this exercise was awkward at first, it helped me build the necessary self-awareness to improve and grow in effectively delivering my message. It also helped me relax and not take myself so seriously.

To be your happiest at work and in life, you need to have self-awareness built in a compassionate and non-judgmental way. This begins with taking a close and loving look in the mirror to see yourself and your life clearly. While working towards getting that feedback and gaining that clarity, don't go down the rabbit hole of over-analyzing the problem, or fall into the trap of creating or believing disempowering stories about why things are the way they are. Instead focus on actionable steps to move you forward. We will talk more about this in a bit, but first things first. Let's start building that self-awareness.

The illusion of "balance" during hybrid and remote work

The idea that work/life balance is the answer to our struggles has been preached for a long time. I even used to buy into it myself, which ultimately led to a lot of guilt and a feeling that I like to call "not-enoughness." Many remote and hybrid workers feel stretched too thinly, like there isn't enough time in the day, which can often leave you feeling like you aren't bringing your A game at work and at home. To a hybrid or remote worker trying to juggle their career, their personal life, and their family, all under the same roof, the concept of finding "balance" can bring on a sense of anxiety and an inner feeling of "I'm not doing enough," and maybe even "I am not enough." To explore this topic more deeply, I ran a poll on LinkedIn where I asked the question, "Does the idea of striving for work/life balance make you feel stressed, uncomfortable, or guilty?" Almost half, 47% of respondents, chose "yes."

Checkpoint

How does the idea of work/life balance make you feel?

The truth is, life is far from perfectly balanced for most individuals. In fact, it's not even balanceable, especially if you are working remotely while simultaneously juggling the many complex layers of life. If you are feeling overwhelmed or guilty about certain areas in your life, it does not mean you are a failure, it means you are human. Everyone experiences feelings of stress and inadequacy to one degree or another at times in work and in life, so let go of the shame and recognize that there is not one perfect way to navigate it all.

Now this idea of "balance" may have been more practical back before computers and cell phones were mainstream, but once your boss, clients, and family all gained unfettered access to you at all times via text, email, and phone, "balance" was placed on shaky ground. Now throw in the context of hybrid and remote work in addition to the chaos and upset the COVID-19 pandemic caused and I'd even say that work/life balance is in quicksand—it's sinking rapidly and there's no saving it. It is just not realistic in modern-day life.

Life was very different back in the 1980s when I was growing up. It was a lot simpler when crimped hair was in style and dancing to Madonna songs was the thing to do. If you grew up in that era, you probably remember having to call a friend on a landline to make plans. No texting, no instant messaging, and definitely no Google. Your parents or siblings could even sneakily listen in on your call if they were quiet enough to pick up another phone in the house. Sure, sometimes it was awkward, but it was also wonderfully simple because there were fewer distractions.

To take a look back in time, in 1984, only 8.2% of US households reported having a computer.[1] (My kids can't believe that I didn't get my first cell phone and computer until I was in college.) Now fast forward to modern times where the majority of people have handheld computers with them at all times. In 2021, 85% of US adults owned a smartphone, and as of January 2024, 5.04 billion, or 62.3% of the world's population, used social media.[2] People are so used to always having phones on them that there is even something called Phantom Vibration Syndrome. I know it kind of sounds like the name of a villain from a superhero movie, but it is really when people experience imaginary phone vibrations.

Now, in addition to the constant attention grab of our cell phones, our homes have become our offices. There's the laundry that's piling up, the dishes left in the sink, not to mention the people in our family lives and our work lives who rely on us throughout the day. The increasing wave of hybrid and remote work brought with it blurred boundaries and challenges resulting in unique struggles.

Back when the COVID-19 pandemic was in full swing, I was talking with a friend about the challenges of having young kids at home while working remotely and she shared a funny and slightly mortifying story. She was on a very important Zoom meeting with some colleagues as well as the head of her company. She was a newer addition to the team and she really wanted to make a great impression. She also had her kids (who didn't care so much about Mommy's agenda) in a neighboring room. After contributing to the work conversation, she hastily hit the mute button to tell her child, who was yelling in the background, to knock it off. Feeling aggravated, she stepped away from her computer, opened the door, and yelled something like "BE QUIET! I'm on an important meeting with my boss!" When she came back to her screen, she immediately knew something was off. The mute button was not on. Everyone on the call had heard her yelling for her child to be quiet. Such was the life of a parent working from home in the middle of a global pandemic. Thankfully, she had a great team that was able to laugh it off with her and it resulted in a funny story to tell that many others could relate to. But that didn't take away the initial shock and embarrassment she felt.

With many organizations and companies switching to hybrid and remote work for the foreseeable future, there is a dire need for long-term solutions to handle the blurred boundaries, potential isolation, and other challenges that can come with remote work.

Checkpoint

How are you handling the added pressures of maintaining productivity and professionalism with your home life being under the same roof as your work life?

With the pulls on you while you are trying to be in "work mode," it's no surprise you might be feeling a little overwhelmed and stressed. And yet, we still pretend that a work/life balance model is the answer to happiness and fulfillment, even with all the changes and added stressors that come with hybrid and remote work. But really, think about it: How many people do you know that truly work nine-to-five anymore? Even if you follow this schedule, do family and personal time happen only between 5:01 p.m. and 8:59 a.m.? Does work matter only between the hours of nine-to-five? The answer is probably "No."

In reality, life is messy and it does not fit neatly into tidy little boxes that are easy to balance. Without intention and a clear roadmap, hybrid and remote work can be tricky to navigate. Trying to leave work at work, making sure to attend important family events, and using your vacation days are no longer enough. Sure, those things are still important, but having lived through a global pandemic, you might be wanting and even *craving* more. We're going to tap into some ancient healing modalities, such as meditation and mindfulness, as well as the new science of microbreaks to create an original, personalized, thoroughly modern approach to your unique work/life situation. By identifying your unique personal mission and your values, you will be able to start living a more meaningful and inspired life while letting go of the guilt that may have surfaced for you in the past.

Urgent! The need for a new wellness model for hybrid and remote work

The COVID-19 pandemic exposed a lot about our society, including the fact that the idea of "perfect balance" is an illusion. How is the typical remote worker going to find the perfect allocation of time for work, family, *and* themselves?

According to data from 2022 shared in an article via Zippia,[3] 86% of employees working remotely full-time experienced burnout, 67% of remote workers felt pressure to be constantly available, and 51% of remote workers didn't feel they were supported by their employer to deal with burnout. These percentages are startling. There is a strong need—even an urgency—for a new model to help hybrid and remote workers thrive personally, professionally, and in their home lives.

Concerns about stress, performance, retention, and happiness at work are not isolated to just one region. This is a global issue. According to Gallup's State of the Global Workplace: 2023 report,[4] which shares data from 2022, globally more than half (51%) of employees said they were actively looking or watching out for a new job. This report also showed that employee stress continued to be at record highs, with East Asia tying Canada and the US for the highest stress levels at 52%. Remote workers and younger workers in East Asia took the unwanted prize of being the most stressed workers worldwide, and the US took the spot for the highest percentage of females regionally with high levels of daily stress.

Taking a closer look at stress levels in different regions, the percentage of workers from Australia and New Zealand that reported a lot of stress in their prior day was 47%, those from Sub-Saharan Africa were at 46%, the Middle East and North Africa were at 45%, Latin America and the Caribbean were at 41%, Europe was at 39%, South Asia at 35%, Southeast Asia at 26%, and post-Soviet Eurasia at 24%. When looking at engagement at work, Europe had the lowest regional percentage of engagement, with just 13% being reported as engaged and thriving at work, while 72% were reported as quiet quitting. Within Europe, the UK had a staggering score for engagement of just 10%.

Looking at the emotion of anger, South Asia came in with the highest percentage of daily anger at 36%, with the Middle East and North Africa coming in second at 32%. It is clear that the current setup for many employees and employers around the world isn't working.

For decades, self-help experts have preached the idea that work/life balance is the answer to feeling fulfilled as we manage our struggles. I used to buy into it myself. Back in 2018, while I was practicing in integrative psychiatry and seeing complex patients on a regular basis, I was also showing up for my husband, my two young kids, and my mother, who was dealing with stage four lung cancer. I was able to effectively juggle this for a while, but with the repeated intense patient cases and the stress of my mother's condition, I began to find it difficult to hold up even an illusion of work/life balance. I found myself feeling stressed and anxious, like I was wearing an invisible backpack which carried the heaviness of my workday into my home life and family time. I felt unable to truly unplug.

I thought the answer was to try to cut back the hours that I was seeing patients. Perhaps increasing my self-care would help? I adjusted my hours and created the "perfect" balance of working in the morning, then picking up my kids in the early afternoon to do all the "mom" stuff that I wanted. I had time to exercise and to meditate. While on paper it looked as though I had great balance from a time perspective, it didn't feel like it. The intensity, pressure, heaviness, and context of my time at work were sticking with me, even with my new hours. I eventually realized that feeling fulfilled wasn't really about the *amount of time* I was spending on these different activities, it was about *my energy and the quality of those moments*: whether they were depleting or nourishing me.

During that time, after intentionally carving out moments for positive self-reflection on what really mattered to me and what I wanted out of work and life, I realized it was time to make a big change so that I could follow the purpose and guidance I felt in my heart. I decided to take a leap and I left clinical practice to enter into the speaking and media space with my company Live Greatly. I actually spend more hours "working" now than at my previous position, but I feel happier, and I have greater fulfillment since work has become an expression of me and my purpose. I have work/life harmony and inner balance now, which is what I had really been searching for all along.

By making this career change, I felt more grounded being there for my mom and my family, and I felt my work and life were more in alignment with my personal mission. My mom passed away in January of 2021, which was (and still is) incredibly difficult, but I am so very thankful for the time that I had with her. When you have those really big, really hard, life experiences, they lead to a lot of soul-searching and reflection. They also put things into perspective and can make a lot of the day-to-day worries, like fear of judgment and fear of rejection, seem insignificant in the big picture. Each day is truly a gift, and it is up to you to make the most of it.

Give yourself permission to be happy now.

The happiest hybrid and remote workers I know don't have perfect external balance in their work and home lives. What they do have is a strong sense of meaning and purpose in what they do, and it impacts how they show up. They know who they are and what really matters to them. They aren't afraid of failure, and they adapt with the circumstances of life, making changes as needed, learning and growing along the way. This helps them have an inner balance that leads to visible happiness and an ease that is apparent even during the most chaotic times. They laugh more when facing life's inevitable challenges. They make the most of the moments they are given. When you get into this empowering mind-set, you trust that you can handle whatever life throws at you, making the journey much less stressful and much more fun.

Creating work/life harmony and a sense of inner balance does not happen overnight. It's an ongoing process. But with practice, you'll be supported in navigating life's ups and downs from a place of internal calm and confidence. By compassionately building self-awareness and getting clear on what truly matter to you, you will have a guide to take the necessary actions for your personal and professional growth and fulfillment.

It's time to wake up

Are you living a life you truly want or one you've been told you should want? You could have been told what career path to pursue by a family member or friend, or led to think certain things would make you happy based on society's messaging, but in the end those things might not have measured up to what you were hoping for. If this resonates with you a little or a lot, you are not alone. The good news here is that every moment is an opportunity to choose again. Working remotely is an incredible chance to fine-tune your personal and professional life so that it is meaningful and fulfilling to you. While I was chatting on my podcast with Evan Carmichael, a popular YouTuber, he shared his unique perspective on burnout, saying, "I think one of the biggest causes of burnout is when people just don't love the work they're doing."

Checkpoint

Do you love the work you are doing?

Sometimes we think something is going to be great or it is going to make us feel a certain way, but the reality is much different than we had envisioned. That's okay. That's a part of life and growth. If you are not happy with where you are at, here's the thing . . . you don't need to be stuck. You get to change your mind if something isn't working. You can approach things in a new way. Think about what you thought you wanted to be when you were a kid and how that has changed over the course of your life with your expanded experiences and interests. Perhaps you wanted to be a singer or a veterinarian or something totally unique. When I was a kid, I went to a Catholic school, and I loved the movie from the 1940s, *The Song of Bernadette*. I also loved animals, so there were two things I really wanted to do: I wanted to teach sign language to monkeys and I also wanted to be a nun. It makes me laugh when I look back on it now, but to eight-year-old Kristel those two career paths were solid options.

In the business of everyday work and life, you may have become disconnected from the things that really bring you joy. You could be lacking awareness and clarity about what is really important and meaningful to you. Without this key self-awareness, you can get stuck living your life based on someone else's version of what is supposed to make you happy. You truly deserve so much more. Developing this self-awareness is the first step to thriving in all areas of your life. Once you have it, you can take the necessary action for positive growth and fulfillment. Now remember, while building this awareness, always be kind to yourself. Be your own biggest advocate and supporter.

Checkpoint

Are you being kind to yourself?

Here is a quick Loving-Kindness Meditation to help you develop self-love and forgiveness:

- Sit quietly in a comfortable spot.
- Close your eyes and soften your breath.
- Repeat the phrase in your mind: "May I be at peace, may I be happy, may I be healthy, may I be loved."
- Now picture a loved one and say in your mind: "May you be at peace, may you be happy, may you be healthy, may you be loved."
- Now picture someone with whom you have had recent tension or frustration. It could be a colleague, family member,

neighbor, whoever, and say in your mind: "May you be at peace, may you be happy, may you be healthy, may you be loved."

• Repeat as desired.

Discovering your personal mission

Each of us has innate things that light us up and get us excited. It could be going to a farmer's market, playing a sport, being with your kids, traveling, helping others, a Taylor Swift song on the radio (no judgment here), gardening, reading—the list is endless! However, when life gets hectic (as it does), sometimes these things get forgotten or brushed to the side.

My husband, Brian, has an innate need to challenge himself with competition, so the thing he needs to fuel this fire is sports. He was a rower in college, competed on the national team, and then ended up playing in a social basketball league post college. After becoming a father and having repeated back injuries that left him down and out for a day or two after each basketball game, he threw in the towel and spent the next six to seven years focusing on our family and his career. He shared with me at one point that he felt like part of his spark was missing without sports as an outlet. After moving to an area where platform tennis was popular, we decided to give it a try. Six years later, he now plays multiple days a week and he has made a ton of great friends through the sport. He even won the club championship at one point, which, in case you're interested, meant he got a personalized mug and some high fives. Most importantly, he found a way to fulfill his unique need for

15

challenge, achievement, and community, all of which come with sports.

To truly thrive in work and life, you need to know what areas of your life are important and meaningful to you. But how do you know what those things are? You are probably pretty clear on the importance of your morning coffee or tea to get you going (if you don't consume any caffeine, I really believe you are superhuman), but what about the bigger things and deeper layers that make you unique? What really fuels your fire? You may have heard people talk about knowing your "why." This means knowing and being clear about your purpose, what inspires you, what motivates you, and *why* you are doing what you are doing. When you are clear on your "why" and what drives you, you will be able to make decisions with more clarity and ease. You will understand where you should dedicate your time and energy for maximum fulfillment, and you will know what needs to shift when you are feeling unfulfilled.

Something that has been brought up in multiple discussions with various experts on my Live Greatly podcast, though said in different ways, is the importance of connecting your everyday activities to the things that are meaningful to you. If you don't see how something will benefit you, or if you don't enjoy something, you most likely aren't going to want to do it. It is important to assign meaningful value to what you do and to find creative ways to add excitement and purpose back into your work/life. I remember a time when Brian and I were trying to teach our children to read and we were struggling to get our son excited about it. We discovered that the key was to get him books about Pokémon. When it was time to read Pokémon books, there wasn't the pushback that we were used to, and he was excited about seeing his favorite characters. As an adult, you can do the same thing for your hybrid or remote workday and your everyday life. What is your Pokémon?

Many people don't even know where to start this self-exploration, let alone land on any answers. This is where the following exercises can help. Through examining what's important to you, you will understand how to add more depth and meaning to your life. Once you awaken to your personal values, you will have the knowledge you need to understand what to incorporate into your daily activities and into your career for maximum fulfillment. You can also get creative with looking into how your values are being represented in your work and your life. For example, if you are someone who has family as a main value and you feel guilty about working, in addition to making sure that you are prioritizing time with family you should get clear on how your work activities help you provide for and support your family. Recognize how the income you are bringing in from work allows your family to have the resources they need. See that, through your career, you are teaching your children important lessons about responsibility and bringing value to the world.

If achievement and financial prosperity are important to you and you are in a career where you feel stifled, focus on how the skills you are learning currently can benefit you in your larger career goals. While I was talking on my podcast with Jason Feifer, editor in chief of *Entrepreneur* magazine, he shared that every job he had wasn't about the job itself, it was about the skills that it taught him. He said that early in his career he stopped thinking about a linear path and started thinking about something deeper—skill sets. You can do this too. If you shift your perspective, you can start to notice all the positive skills you are learning and then become intentional with how they can help launch you to where you want to land. If family and career advancement are important to you and you struggle with self-care, you could benefit from recognizing how activities like taking regular breaks and exercising support your health and vitality. By prioritizing those things, you will have higher-quality energy to spend time with loved ones. You will also have improved focus at work, all while hopefully living a longer, healthier life.

Have you ever encountered someone working at a coffee shop or a grocery store who seems to thoroughly enjoy their job, and their contentment and enthusiasm rub off on you? I had that experience recently when I went to buy an Americano at a café. The cashier welcomed me with a genuine smile and seemed to be radiating excitement about his life. When he asked me how my day was going, I felt like he really wanted to know. It seemed to me that working the register at that coffee shop was the only place he wanted to be at that moment, and he was rocking it. Maybe he wanted to have a lifelong career as a barista, maybe he was making some side money to put himself through school, or maybe he was polishing his social skills with the end goal of getting into politics. Regardless of his intentions, it was clear that he was doing something in alignment with what was meaningful to him, and that optimism rubbed off on me.

As human beings, we are influenced and impacted by others (see Figure 1.1), and for better or worse, emotions can actually be contagious. There is even a scientific name for this: emotional contagion.[5] After my interaction with the barista that day, I walked out feeling inspired, because that's the impact people have when they are doing things that light them up. That's what happens when you know what is important to you and you find deeper meaning and purpose in your career and life.

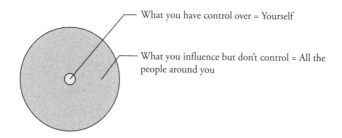

What you have control over = Yourself

What you influence but don't control = All the people around you

Figure 1.1 Control and influence

Personal values exercise

Are you ready to peel back the layers of guilt and uncertainty to figure out what really matters to you? I hereby grant you permission to be a little bit selfish in the absolute best sense of the word. It's time to let go of others' expectations of you to figure out what you really want and desire.

Once you take time to really know yourself, you can start showing up as the best version of you in all areas of your work/life. The following exercises will help you gain an understanding of your unique personal values, while getting clear on the critical components that you need to integrate into your day and your life for sustained fulfillment and happiness. They will help you begin to have awareness around what should be taking up less of your time, and where you should be focusing more of your time and energy. You can use these values to bring more meaning and depth into your workday by thinking about how they can be more fully represented in your daily choices and activities. When you have clarity about what is meaningful to you, making larger life decisions becomes easier. It's time for you to start uncovering your personal mission.

Step 1: Find a comfortable and peaceful space where you can reflect on what is meaningful to you. Put a Do Not Disturb sign on your door if you need to, or go to a quiet area outside. Have a pen and notebook on hand.

Step 2: Ask yourself the following questions, reflect on them, and then write down your answers. Make sure you are being honest and not just saying what you think you are supposed to say.

o When was the last time you felt truly happy? What were you doing then and what was happening in your life?
o What are things that spark natural joy in you?
o What would you do for free?
o If you won the lottery and money was never an issue for you again, what would you want to fill your days and life with?
o What are some common things people regularly compliment you on?
o What are some things that friends, family, or colleagues always come to you for?

- ○ What are you naturally interested in and would love to learn more about?
- ○ If you got to arrange the perfect day, what would that look like?
- ○ Which areas do you wish you had more time for?
- ○ What makes you feel empowered and happy in your job?
- ○ When are you most productive?
- ○ When was the last time you felt really great about your career path?
- ○ When was the last time you felt really great about your relationships?
- ○ When was the last time you felt really healthy and energized?

Step 3: Now that you have more awareness around what is meaningful to you and what contributes to you having a fulfilling life, take out a piece of paper and write the word "ME" in the center and circle it. Picture yourself feeling happy, healthy, and confident. Then write down the things that are most important to you around the word "ME." Include the top things that give you and your work and life meaning and purpose. There are many different core values lists out there and there are tons of possibilities here! Some examples could be achievement, community, creativity, faith, family, freedom, friends, fun, health, leadership, money, recognition, or travel.

Step 4: Now that you have a clearer understanding of your values, take some time to reflect on the following questions.

o Is your list of values appropriately represented by how you spend your time?

o Is your current career in alignment with your personal values? If not, where is there room for improvement?

o Are your relationships in alignment with your values? If not, where is there room for improvement?

o Are your personal life and your relationship with yourself in alignment with your core values? If not, where is there room for improvement?

o How can your core values be better represented in your career, relationships, and personal choices?

Step 5: Take out a piece of paper and a pen. Write "Time Suckers" in the middle of the page and circle it. Now draw a line from that center circle and write down something that is draining your time. Continue this process until you feel you have written down the main issues that are taking your energy away from things that are meaningful to you. Some examples could be scrolling on your phone, checking social media, poor organization, unnecessary meetings. Now that these time suckers have been identified, you can start making the necessary adjustments to more appropriately manage your time to include the things that truly matter to you.

Take a moment to give yourself a pat on the back and be proud of yourself for taking the time to make your happiness, well-being, and success a priority. Allow yourself to release the guilt, let go of striving for perfect "balance," and instead aim to have a fulfilling and meaningful work/life.

By incorporating the insights gained from these exercises and the knowledge in the pages ahead, you will continue to support yourself in having a successful career, joyful relationships, and a fun life filled with the unique things that matter most to you.

Endnotes

1 U.S. Bureau of the Census (1988) *Computer Use in the United States: 1984.* www.census.gov/history/pdf/computerusage1984.pdf

2 Petrosyan, A. (2024) *Worldwide digital population 2024.* www.statista.com/statistics/617136/digital-population-worldwide/#:~:text=Worldwide%20digital%20population%202023&text=As%20of%20July%202023%2C%20there,population%2C%20were%20social%20media%20users

3 McCain, A. (2023) *25 crucial remote work burnout statistics [2023]: How to recognize and avoid workplace stress.* www.zippia.com/advice/remote-work-burnout-statistics/

4 Gallup, Inc. (2023) *State of the Global Workplace.* www.gallup.com/workplace/349484/state-of-the-global-workplace.aspx?thank-you-report-form=1, accessed 1 May 2023.

5 Psychology Today (n.d.) *Emotional Contagion.* www.psychologytoday.com/us/basics/emotional-contagion

CHAPTER 2

Stop tripping yourself up

● ● ●

When was the last time you intentionally made yourself trip while walking or dancing? Unless you were trying to make a funny video, your answer is probably "never." While this may sound ridiculous, we trip ourselves up and limit ourselves all the time with our internal dialogue. I'm going to ask you a question and I want you to be completely honest with yourself about it . . . *Is your inner voice more of a best friend or more of a bully?*

For many of us, our inner voice can be a little bit of both depending on the day or the situation. If things are going well in your life or you just received positive feedback, that inner voice is probably cheering you on, saying things like "You've got this!" or "That was brilliant!" However, if things haven't been working out the way you had hoped, if you made a mistake, or if you received negative feedback, then what happens? Does that inner bully pop in, making you feel like a failure? That inner voice saying, "I'm not good enough." "That was so stupid." "I'm too old." These thoughts and beliefs can plague even the most successful people.

When I think back to my 20s, before I had ventured down the road of self-awareness and personal development, I had a lot of inner dialogue that without me realizing it was limiting me and keeping me stuck. From beliefs like "I could never start my own business" and "I am bad at public speaking" to ideas like "It is selfish taking time for myself" and "It's my job to make other people happy."

One key thing that I've learned from working with patients with extremely successful careers, as well as talking to many incredible individuals throughout my life, is that even people that seem to be living perfect lives have their unique struggles, and many have dealt with or are currently dealing with self-limiting beliefs. When I was working in integrative psychiatry, I had people come into the office that on paper seemed to have it all. They checked all the boxes for what the world tells us success looks like. Beauty, check. Money, check. Power, check. Prestige, check. But here's the thing, many of these individuals were not happy, and many were dealing with insecurities and a lack of meaning and fulfillment in their lives.

Matt Higgins, who wrote the foreword for this book, has shared that he himself has dealt with imposter syndrome. When Matt was a guest on my Live Greatly podcast, he talked about how he was backstage before going on the show *Shark Tank* when Daymond John said to him, "Don't let anyone tell you that you don't belong here. You belong here because you *are* here."

If you've ever stepped outside of your comfort zone, thoughts and feelings of insecurity, doubt, and uncertainty are probably familiar. I remember when I was giving a keynote talk to a large group of people for a prestigious company and I felt a significant amount of pressure to have it be my best keynote yet. After a lot of preparation, I went into the talk feeling confident, with my inner voice cheering me on. When I walked off stage, I felt I had nailed it. The audience engagement was great. I received a large amount of applause as I left and some people in the audience approached me after my talk to tell me how much they enjoyed it.

Not long after the talk, I reached out to the event coordinator via email asking for feedback. Fast forward three days when I was back in the comfort of my own home and I received a response. They thanked me for speaking at their event and then they shared results from an anonymous survey that they had taken among the members of the audience after my talk. Now there is something about receiving feedback that can make you feel like a deer in headlights. Suddenly you feel like the flashlight is placed on you, flaws and all, and a vulnerability can surface. In this situation, I started nervously looking through the results of the survey and I saw many great responses from people in the audience where they said things like, it was my favorite talk, I learned so much, and other positive feedback. As I continued to read and scroll down, I felt my clenched muscles slightly relax, leaving me relieved and happy with what I had seen so far.

And then I came across a comment that stopped me in my tracks. This audience member said something about my talk being *a waste of their time*, without giving any specifics or suggestions for improvement. As soon as I read those words, I felt insecurity and doubt swoop in. My inner voice that had been cheering me on a moment before started to question my abilities and my skill sets. I found myself thinking things like, oh my gosh, I thought it had gone really well, was I actually bad up there? I took a few moments to compose myself and I finished reading the rest of the results, which were overwhelmingly positive, with a couple of constructive suggestions which I appreciated. But even after seeing how many people felt inspired after my talk, I still felt shaken up from that one solo comment, so I decided to go out for a walk to try to clear my head and get a new perspective. When I returned, I felt slightly better, but there was still a lingering feeling of hurt and disappointment, so I walked into my husband's office and told him about the situation. He smiled at me and said, you are missing the big picture here. Look at how many people said that hearing you speak helped them. Don't let the opinion of one person make you lose sight of all the good you are doing. And remember, you can't make everyone happy all the time. Who knows what that person was going through or what headspace they were in. That comment most likely had absolutely nothing to do with you. His insight helped me gain the perspective I needed. I had let that inner bully creep in, which had created self-doubt, but I decided at that moment to embrace the inner voice that had my back, that was focused on progress and not perfection—and you can too.

Now, it's not a surprise that even though I had received a lot of wonderful feedback in that survey, my focus and attention attached to that one response with a negative thing to say. As human beings, our brains are hardwired to notice the negative more than the positive, which is suggested to be an evolutionary effort to try to keep us safe. This is called the negativity bias[1] and knowing about it is the first step to being able to successfully navigate it. People tend to place more value on and give more weight to the negative things they see, hear, and encounter than the positive. This can impact you in all areas of your work and life because it influences how you interpret the world, how you feel, and ultimately the decisions you make.

Have you ever had a day that started off with something going wrong, then for the rest of the day it felt like the world was against you? Maybe you spilled coffee on yourself first thing and then you ended up being late for a meeting. Later on, you had a stressful interaction with your boss or a client. The list went on and on. So, what's really behind these "bad" days? Is it the events themselves, or is it how we are interpreting them? Here's the thing: while there are bound to be days where unexpected hiccups happen, if your brain is primed to put more focus on the negative, like the coffee you spilled, it will keep looking for more "negative" things to bring to your attention, potentially blowing them out of proportion, while mostly disregarding the positive things happening simultaneously. The lens through which you will be viewing your interactions and experiences can be skewed. So, knowing humans' tendencies towards the negativity bias can help you see those "bad" days in a new light. On days when you spill your coffee, are running late, or have an uncomfortable encounter at work, recognize that there are also many things going well or even great along the way, you just need to be more intentional to seek them out and notice them.

Checkpoint

How is the negativity bias impacting you in your everyday work and life?

Think back to when you were a teenager and you had a pimple on your face. Whenever you looked in the mirror, your attention probably went right to it, and it might have seemed there was a mountain on your face instead of a small bump. You most likely thought that every person you talked to would end up staring right at it, when in reality most people probably wouldn't even notice it at all, and if they did, they would likely glance at it and their attention would quickly shift elsewhere. If you are laser focused on something, it can become larger than it really is. You need to zoom out to really see the big picture with a clear view.

Embrace your missteps

Our self-talk is a powerful tool that can impact all areas of our lives. If you go into a situation doubting yourself, it can negatively impact your performance. Now, it's completely normal and 100% okay to be nervous and uncertain sometimes, but you need to be able to trust in yourself and your abilities along the way. That said, even if you have the best intentions of going into a situation with an empowering mindset, there will be times when your inner critic makes a surprise visit.

I recently experienced this exact situation after joining a new women's tennis team. It had started out better than I had expected. I was having a lot of fun, and I was playing well with a new doubles partner. A couple months in we had some great wins under our belts, and when the rosters for the upcoming matches came out, we were slotted on a higher court than we had been in the past. I went into that match excited for the tougher competition and I was feeling confident. However, I then remembered that I was a newbie to tennis. I had taken one tennis lesson as a kid, and I swung at the air so many times, missing the ball, that I left that lesson feeling mortified. Could I really hold my own on this higher court? I started out playing okay in the match and we were in the lead, which helped, but then I missed an easy shot. And then I missed another shot . . . suddenly, I felt fear and self-doubt creep in. I started over-thinking my strokes. I found myself feeling afraid that I would miss. I wondered, had my great shots prior to this all been a fluke? Maybe I wasn't good enough to be on this higher court? My partner and I went from being well in the lead to being tied.

At that point, I decided that I needed to shift my mind-set and adjust my internal story. I told myself that I just needed to go for it and if I missed, that was okay. I realized that I had started playing timidly, like I was afraid to miss, afraid to lose, instead of being relaxed and confident. I was putting pressure on myself to be perfect, and that wasn't realistic or helpful. Once I became aware of this, I gave myself permission to miss and there was a big turnaround. I was able to get back on track and I started playing as I had hoped I would.

Checkpoint

Is being afraid to fail preventing you from performing at your best and getting into a flow state? You know that you are in a flow state when you become fully engrossed in an activity with enjoyable attentive focus.

No one is perfect. You are going to miss sometimes in your personal and professional life and that is 100% okay! Adjust, adapt, and keep taking your shots.

Gain clarity

When you are looking to move past limiting beliefs and patterns, building self-awareness is important, but it is just as important that you are going about it in a way that is empowering for you. Sometimes introspection can be started with good intentions, but if it's not done in a productive way, it can suck you down into a rabbit hole of ruminating and getting down on yourself. To avoid this, take a look at where things are objectively and with compassion, acknowledge them, and then focus on what you can do to move in the direction you really want to go in. Be future focused, looking for insights, such as *what* can I do to get to where I want to be, instead of focusing on something like, *why* are things not going well for me? You will learn more specifics around how to best navigate introspection and build awareness in the section "Building awareness, emotional intelligence, and empathy" in Chapter 8. If you are looking for support in navigating this, there are many counseling, coaching, and therapy options out there that can help.

Another thing that can support your well-being is getting clear on mutually beneficial relationships. Surrounding yourself with people that are in your corner can help support positive self-talk and an uplifting mindset. While discussing this with Dr. Michelle King (PhD), who is a researcher and inequality and organizational culture expert, she shared that the most stressful relationships are actually the ambiguous ones. On my podcast, Michelle said, "What research finds is, if we're not sure if somebody has our back, it can create a lot of anxiety and stress for us." Surprisingly, Michelle then went on to say, "It's not people who are negative. So, if you know there is somebody on your team who is a bit negative, doesn't really have your back, tends to be unhelpful, actually knowing that alleviates the stress. It's the people where it's ambiguous. It's the people where we're not sure, right? Because we spend a huge amount of mental energy trying to work out how to manage them, are they on my team, are they not? I can't quite tell." We've all had the experience of running into someone we know and having them say that they would love to get together and they will reach out to set something up and then you don't hear from them. These situations can be confusing. You may find yourself thinking, did they really want to get together or were they just saying that to be polite?

When it comes down to it, you can't control other people, but you can control your response to them. You are giving away your power and hurting yourself if you spend your time and energy trying to solve the unsolvable. You will never truly know 100% of what people feel or think or why they acted the way they did. You only really know your interpretations. Instead of focusing on these things, put your mental energy and time towards developing strong self-encouragement and positive behaviors that reinforce your core values and your aspirations. With patience and positive self-encouragement, you can begin to develop and reinforce a growth mindset and inner dialogue that support your health, happiness, success, and work/life harmony wherever you work.

It's time for a new dance

Have you ever driven to a familiar destination and realized that along the way you didn't need to think at all about where you were going? Your body took over, automatically knowing where to turn, where to go, just like you were on autopilot. Similarly, our thoughts and habitual reactions can be on autopilot mode, resulting in repeated thought patterns, feelings, and behaviors that may or may not serve us. If you were cruising down the expressway heading some-place you go to on a weekly or daily basis, you most likely wouldn't notice or pay attention to the many exits along the highway. You would zoom right past them, focused solely on your predetermined destination, and many of those exits might not even be in your awareness at all. The same thing can happen with our thoughts, feelings, and actions. We can get stuck doing the same things, thinking the same way, repeating the same behaviors, programed to get to the same destination over and over, keeping us from true fulfillment and success.

Now what if one day when you were speeding down the highway to your pre-programed destination, you noticed an exit on the highway you hadn't been aware of before and found it piqued your interest. On a whim you decided to get off on that exit and you drove around a bit. As you looked out your window you realized that you really loved the neighborhood. You felt different there. Happier. More invigorated. More inspired. You even found yourself think-ing about what it would be like to live there, a move which could change the trajectory of your entire life. Now, the same thing is possible if you build compassionate awareness around your habitual thought patterns, beliefs, feelings, and actions. Doing this creates the possibility of *intentionally choosing a new exit* that better suits you.

Cognitive Behavioral Therapy is a type of psychological therapy which incorporates something called the cognitive triangle (see Figure 2.1). Our thoughts, feelings, and behaviors all impact one another, and a lot of the time we aren't even aware of it. A key thing to recognize here is that a lot of our thoughts are simply not true. Sure, many thoughts are based on facts or observations, but many are also utter nonsense. Some are outright lies. Others are based on limiting beliefs and stories keeping us stuck. Some may be fear-based "what if" scenarios and others may be interpretations or opinions based on your personal perspective, again not facts. Now if you believe all or most of your thoughts, this will have a strong influence on how you feel and how you act. For better or worse, this can impact you in all areas of your personal and professional life.

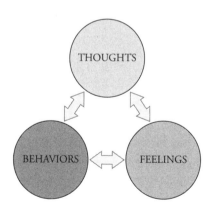

Figure 2.1 The cognitive triangle

Things get really interesting when you start to realize that you don't need to believe all of your thoughts or limiting beliefs. You can intentionally choose to influence this triangle by building awareness and then introducing more empowering behaviors to support more uplifting beliefs about yourself. You could choose an action that is in alignment with a belief you want to have about yourself. You can do things that make you *feel* your best, like exercise, spending time in nature, or being with uplifting friends, which can then have a positive impact on your *thoughts* and *behaviors*. Remember the negativity bias we talked about? You could try introducing new possibilities for how to think about and interpret situations that are more encouraging with reframing, which we will get into in a bit. There are a lot of resources out there to support you. If you are concerned about or are struggling with your mental health, make sure to always reach out to a mental health professional for guidance and support.

Have you ever felt vulnerable or nervous about sending a text message or an email to someone that you wanted to connect with? It could have been a friend you hadn't talked to in a while, someone new you wanted to get to know better, or maybe a colleague you were reaching out to. After getting up the courage to click the "send" button, you nervously waited for a response and then . . . crickets. Nothing. No response. When situations like this occur, it is kind of like you are the main character in your personal choose-your-own-adventure storybook.

You could choose option A: Feel sorry for yourself, doubt yourself, and think about all the possible reasons why this person may not like you. This response may negatively influence your feelings and behaviors, and it could keep you from putting yourself out there in future scenarios. You could choose option B: Acknowledge that you can't really know the real reason why this person didn't respond. Be proud of yourself for trying and think about other relationships that you could focus on building or strengthening, which may be more mutually beneficial.

Now even if you have historically chosen something like option A, other options are always available to you. Remember, you can always choose a new exit.

Three steps to a more empowered you in your work/life

Is there an area in your life where you feel restricted? If the answer is "Yes," you are likely harboring some beliefs that are holding you back. By implementing the mindset exercises shared here, you will learn tools to help you navigate negative self-talk to support a mindset that supports you and cheers you on.

The first step to break free of limiting beliefs is to non-judgmentally *become aware* of them. The second step is to create space for a new perspective to emerge by asking yourself *"How can I view this in a way that is more empowering for me?"*. The third step is to *take action*. Choose a small positive thing you can do, which may be outside of your comfort zone, to start the shift to a more empowering belief.

Perhaps you have noticed that when you are working remotely, you don't have as many social interactions and maybe you have found yourself missing in-person contact or feeling lonely. You may even find that you have some limiting beliefs around this area, such as "I can't incorporate fun or social time within my workday" or "It's too hard to have meaningful interactions amid my remote workdays." If you fall into this category, ask yourself how you can view this situation in a new way that is more empowering for you. Then think about ways that you could take action to support a more uplifting view. Perhaps that could mean reaching out to a friend close by or someone that lives in your area who you would like to get to know better to see if they would like to grab lunch or coffee. Maybe you could ask a neighbor if they would like to start going on a regular walk mid-morning or mid-afternoon to take a break from your workload. Or maybe once a week you could go to your local café and get a little work done in a new environment with more people around. Perhaps you could join a new fitness class, club, or group.

Once you begin to introduce a new behavior, a new action, a new choice, you start to reinforce a new, more uplifting view around your ability to have meaningful interactions amid your remote workdays. That then influences how you feel and even how you think. Introducing these new behaviors takes courage and vulnerability, so be proud of yourself for putting yourself out there, regardless of the outcome.

Checkpoint

Where is your internal story holding you back when it comes to your work/life situation?

Another key thing to remember when it comes to our mindset is that sometimes our interpretations of situations can be off. If you have been interacting with someone at work, whether it was your boss or a client on the other end of a Zoom call, it is natural to have opinions about how the other person was feeling and how the conversation went. If the person on the other end was smiling, encouraging, and talkative, you may leave that interaction thinking that they liked you and that things went well. However, if the person on the other end was quiet, unengaging, seemed distracted or irritated, you may leave asking yourself, was it me? Did I do something? Or you may find yourself thinking, they just don't like me for some reason . . . One thing all humans tend to have in common is we make things about ourselves, even if other people's actions or moods have nothing to do with us.

One potential downside to always believing your opinions and interpretations is that they could be completely off base, and they could negatively impact your actions towards that person or others in the future. For example, if you felt that a client didn't like you after an interaction, you may avoid them or respond in an uncomfortable or defensive way during your next meeting. However, there could be many potential reasons this person was acting the way they did; maybe they didn't sleep well the night before, maybe they were dealing with a sick family member, maybe they had social anxiety, maybe they express their emotions differently than you, or maybe they actually really didn't like you for some reason. Regardless, you don't need to spend your time and energy trying to figure it out. Once you recognize this, you can intentionally respond to others in a way that is in alignment with who you want to be, not in a way that is being reactive due to uncertainty or hurt feelings.

This same awareness and higher perspective can be extremely helpful in your personal life as well. I remember when my family and I moved to a new area years ago and I was going out of my way to meet new people. I had met some women in the area and I was excited to have made some friendships early on. Now, there was a specific woman who I was introduced to several times and every time I tried to get her to warm up to me, she didn't seem interested. I went out of my way to talk with her, but she seemed distracted and disengaged. I would see her out and about around town and try to wave hello, and it was like she didn't see me. I was convinced that she didn't like me. I thought she was intentionally trying to avoid me for some reason, and it left me feeling irritated. I noticed that I started feeling annoyed when I saw her, and I began to try to avoid her. Then, surprisingly, months later, we ended up crossing paths and she approached me differently. She seemed excited to get to know me. She started sharing things about herself and her life and I realized that the way she had been acting previously most likely had absolutely nothing to do with me. She had a lot of stress in her work/life and it had been impacting how she showed up. This was a good reminder for me of the importance of keeping a higher perspective and not believing all the stories that we tell ourselves about situations and others. Remember, others' behaviors and moods are not always about you, and while you can't control others, you can control how you respond to them and to the events in your life.

Your mindset impacts everything

While taking the steps discussed above to work towards over-coming your limiting beliefs, you also need to actively nurture a more empowering mindset. One way to do that is to practice mindfulness. You can't actively change things that are beyond your awareness. According to the *Merriam-Webster* dictionary, mindfulness is defined as "the practice of maintaining a nonjudgmental state of heightened or complete awareness of one's thoughts, emotions, or experiences on a moment-to-moment basis."[2] Mindfulness is training your mind to be present. It is about bringing your attention and focus to the present moment and getting curious by starting to recognize your feelings, behaviors, reactions, and responses in different circumstances, free of judgement, and without attaching to the thoughts passing through your mind.

When you build this awareness, you create more space between your thoughts, feelings, and responses. This space helps you have the room to respond differently. Remember, you can always choose a new exit!

Practices that support mindfulness

MEDITATION

I remember when I first heard about meditation years ago and I thought that it was really a spiritual practice meant mostly for monks. That interpretation couldn't be further from the truth. Meditation can be a valuable way for people from all backgrounds, cultures, and situations to de-stress and calm down from the busyness of everyday work and life.

There are many different types of meditation practices out there and I have dabbled in many of them myself. If you would like to begin to explore meditation, there are a couple simple places you could start. One possibility is downloading a meditation app on your phone and following the guided meditation options. Another is to sit comfortably with your back straight and your eyes closed. Focus your attention on your in breath and your out breath. You can think of your breath like waves crashing on a beach, or tree branches blowing softly in the wind. Just breathe in and breathe out through your nose. Thoughts will come— let them pass without investigating them or attaching to them. If your mind wanders, just come back to your in breath and out breath. If you are new to meditation, you can begin doing this exercise for a five-minute time frame and then work up from there.

BODY SCANS

Your body is always in the present moment. When you bring your attention back to your body, you are refocusing on the here and now as well as actively working to reduce the tension being carried in your muscles throughout the day.

To begin a body scan, either lay on the floor or sit comfortably on a chair. If it is safe, you would normally close your eyes, but for the purposes of this exercise, keep your eyes open. Bring your focus and attention down to the tips of your toes. Notice what you feel. Are your toes relaxed or curled up tightly? Gently relax your toes as you bring your focus up your feet to your ankles and then your calves, letting any tension loosen as you go. Continue to bring your attention up your legs to your knees, your thighs, and your hips, noticing if there is any tightness or discomfort in areas. Relax any clenched or tight muscles as you go. Bring your focus to your lower back, your belly, your ribcage, your mid back, upper back, and shoulders. Is your belly relaxed? Are your shoulders raised or tight? Continue to relax your muscles as you go, breathing in and out. Now bring your focus down your arms to your elbows, then to your wrists, hands, and fingers. What sensations do you notice in your hands? Now bring your attention back up your arms and shoulders to your neck, relaxing the back of your neck and then the front of your neck as you go. Continue up your head to your forehead, your cheeks, and your mouth, relaxing your jaw, your tongue, your eyebrows and then your eyes. Notice how your whole body feels. You are vibrantly alive, relaxed, and present.

MINDFUL WALKING

When was the last time you went on a walk without the goal of getting to a certain destination? Oftentimes we walk with the intent of arriving somewhere instead of fully embracing each step and each moment along the way. With mindful walking, the purpose of the walk is to be fully immersed in every single step. Each time your foot touches the ground you are present. This practice can do wonders to calm your mind and boost well-being and performance, while incorporating the benefits of movement. This practice can also be used while walking around the house. Perhaps every time you walk into the kitchen you decide to practice mindful walking. Maybe every time you take the stairs you decide to come back to the present moment and be present in every step. Or maybe every time you need a bathroom break. Don't overcomplicate it but be intentional with it. This is a powerful practice that can easily be used on an everyday basis in your work/life.

MINDFUL EATING

Have you ever eaten your lunch while working and then realized that it was gone before you were able to really notice what everything tasted like? When you eat mindfully, you are choosing to be present for each bite and each sip during your meal. By bringing your attention to the tastes, smells, and textures of your meal you will turn your mealtime and snack time into a reprieve, embracing self-care and nourishment. Creating a ritual where you take a mindful snack or a tea break mid workday can give you a respite that can help you recenter, regroup, and recharge so that you come back to your work with a fresh mind.

STRESS BUSTER

As you go about your workday and your everyday life, one thing is certain: there will be moments of stress. Ups and downs and twists and turns are all part of life's adventures. That said, there are ways to set yourself up to better handle the curveballs that come your way. The stress response[3] is a normal human reaction when we feel threatened or when we are faced with challenges or change. While stress is a part of life, we need to learn how to optimally navigate it. Sustained stress and continued stress without relief can lead to a multitude of health problems.

While adding in intentional, relaxing, and stress-reducing activities is important, managing the stories we create around events in our work/life has a big impact as well. Sometimes the prolonged struggles that can come with stress are more about how we perceive and respond to events and situations in our lives and less about the actual event itself.

Amid your remote or hybrid workday you will likely find that you rely heavily on technology to get your work done. While technology is great for many things, it is not 100% reliable. There will be times when your WiFi signal is low, your computer is glitchy, or an update starts running right as you are trying to log onto an important video meeting. You can do everything in your control to set yourself up for a successful workday, but then something may occur which is outside of your control. When things like this happen, the resistance to what is going on and holding onto your frustration or disappointment may end up being more stressful than the event itself. Think for a moment about how much time and energy you spend being upset about something, dwelling on things like "I can't believe this happened" or "This is so unfair" when all that does is keep you feeling stressed and stuck. Instead of going down that road, let go of the resistance to what is and try this instead:

Allow—let go of pushing against what is.

Accept—it is what it is. Accept the reality of the current moment.

Adapt—what can you do to set yourself up for success given the current situation?

You may find it helpful to say something to yourself during chaotic times, such as "Allow," to remind you to stop resisting the present moment and to work with it instead.

I found myself in a situation where this came in handy while I was preparing to go live for a TV appearance remotely. I was excited, and a bit nervous, as the host came onto the screen to welcome me. My video feed and image were clear as we were talking and then it was time to start rolling. The image on my screen changed as they shifted to record, and I noticed that things started to freeze up and blip on my screen. The host's questions came through slightly delayed but I did my best to stay focused and respond as if things were flowing normally. I was hoping that while things seemed a bit glitchy on my end, perhaps the recording was smooth on theirs. Given the nature of the interview, I didn't have time to over-think it or freak out. I accepted that it was what it was and I did my best to adapt given the circumstances. Once we were done recording, the host and I discussed the technical issues and we decided that we would re-record later that week. In preparation for that TV interview, I went above and beyond to make sure my WiFi signal was 100%. I made the necessary adjustments and the second interview went flawlessly. The next time you find yourself in a stressful situation, do yourself a favor and minimize the stress by allowing, accepting, and adapting.

In my career, I have had great conversations with extremely successful athletes, multi-millionaires, and top CEOs, and there is something I have noticed: they don't let others tell them what is and what is not possible for them. They make their own path based on an internal compass of what is important to *them* and they seek out individuals to support them. Just like everyone else, they feel fear and they deal with failure, but what sets them apart is that they don't let those things stop them. They have a mindset that sets them up for success, and you can too.

While talking on my podcast with Moira Forbes, President and Publisher of ForbesWomen, she shared, "You're braver than you think and you're stronger than you think and you realize, innately it's true, you have so much more in you, I think we all do, than we ever give ourselves credit for or we ever even let ourselves try and understand and realize the potential of." You don't want to look back on your life thinking, "If only I had [fill in the blank]." Now, let's continue to work towards uncovering your full potential.

Limiting belief exercise

Take out a pen and paper and write the word "ME" in the center of the paper with a circle around it. Lovingly reflect on any limiting beliefs you have about yourself and write them out around the word "Me." Now move beyond one limiting belief and write something new and more empowering (see Figure 2.2). An example for someone who didn't feel confident as a leader would be reinterpreting "I am a bad leader" and instead writing "I am working on fine-tuning my leadership skills." Then think about some actionable things you could do today to support that. If you find yourself thinking, "I'm too old," you could shift this to, "I can uncover new skills and passions at any age." If you notice beliefs like, "I am not good enough to do this," you could reframe it to, "If this is something I really want, I can put in the time and effort and learn as I go."

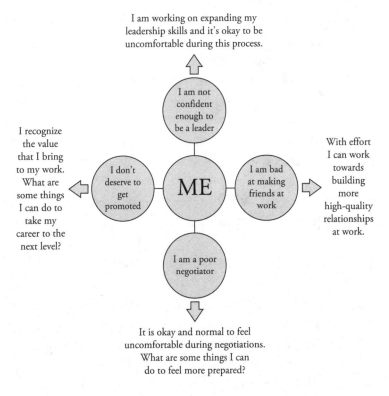

Figure 2.2 Replace limiting beliefs with empowering ones

Endnotes

1 Vaish, A., Grossmann, T. & Woodward, A. (2008) Not all emotions are created equal: The negativity bias in social-emotional development. *Psychol Bull*, 134(3): 383–403. doi: 10.1037/0033-2909.134.3.383. PMID: 18444702; PMCID: PMC3652533. www.ncbi.nlm.nih.gov/pmc/articles/PMC3652533/

2   Merriam-Webster (2024) *Mindfulness.* www.merriam-webster.com/dictionary/mindfulness

3   Cleveland Clinic (2024) *Stress* https://my.clevelandclinic.org/health/articles/11874-stress

CHAPTER 3

Fueling your dance moves

● ● ●

If you want to be at the top of your game in the dance of work and life, you need the proper fuel. I remember when Brian and I decided that we were going to make the switch to an electric car. We researched how far a fully charged electric car could travel without recharging and we took the plunge, deciding to go with a Tesla. Making this transition required some key steps in order to be successful. We needed to have a special outlet installed in our garage for the Tesla charger so that it could safely and efficiently charge. We put a lot of effort into making sure that our new car was plugged in every night so that it was at maximum capacity in the morning. After driving in our new electric car for a while, I realized that the number of estimated miles left on the charge was not always accurate. Different variables like highway driving and weather conditions could impact how quickly the battery drained. I also discovered the magic of superchargers for longer drives which were super-speedy versions of what we had at home. I found that I really enjoyed being able to zoom past gas stations without needing to stop in.

Comparable to a car, your body needs certain types of fuel to help you run at maximum capacity. Just like the differences between electric vehicles and gas-powered cars, each person is unique and will have different needs specific to them. Some fuel will keep you charged for short periods of time only. Other fuel can supercharge you, helping you feel your best throughout a full workday. And certain types of fuel could deplete you and even really hurt you, resulting in you breaking down or worse. Just like there are different variables that impact how quickly a charge on an electric car is depleted, there are stressors, unexpected events and situations that pop up in your personal and professional life which will impact how often you need to refuel and how best to do it. Without regular recharging, care, and attention, your body will not function properly, and your mind can suffer, hindering your well-being and performance. However, with appropriate awareness and choices, you can fine-tune your fueling schedule, making sure that it will keep you running smoothly and happily at peak performance for many years to come.

Avoiding burnout culture

Picture this: Jenny is a stressed-out college student up at 3 a.m., frantically typing on her laptop to finish the last five pages of her twenty-page research paper that's due in her professor's inbox by 7 a.m. She refills her coffee cup while shakily eating a donut, trying to get some fuel however she can to stay awake. She clicks the "send" button at 5 a.m. and gets two and a half hours of sleep before rolling out of bed to make it to her 8 a.m. class. Why is this an unsurprising image? Because from a very early age we are ingrained with the idea that we must sacrifice to be successful.

Back when I was practicing in healthcare and regularly seeing patients, I repeatedly had teenagers and young adults coming in looking for ways to cope with the anxiety and pressure they were feeling trying to live up to the expectations their parents, teachers, and seemingly the whole world had placed on them. It was like their entire life was hanging on the thread of getting an A on their final, which should get them into the best school, resulting in an offer for the perfect job, ultimately leading to happiness and an incredible life. That's how it's supposed to work, right? Not so much . . .

The problem with this early socialization is that many people end up sacrificing their well-being trying to attain a misguided vision of success. This extreme hustle culture mindset can lead straight to a road of unhappiness, poor health, and burnout.

This behavior doesn't end with school. It continues into parenting and careers as well, and even more so with remote work. Remote and hybrid workers are particularly susceptible to these patterns. For example, scheduling back-to-back video meetings without giving yourself a break, skipping lunch due to being overwhelmed with work, brushing aside exercise because you feel guilty taking time away from your family or your career. Working excess hours due to blurred boundaries between your personal and professional life, or sacrificing sleep to finish that last project. The list goes on and on.

Like many people, you may well have fallen into the trap of neglecting your true desires and needs in some areas to fit the mold of what you think the world expects from you. As a remote or hybrid worker, you may be placing even more pressure on yourself to overperform to prove that you aren't slacking off. Here's the thing: this type of lifestyle will only negatively impact your work performance and it's a surefire way to feel dissatisfied in life.

Sacrificing key parts of yourself to please others is always a lose-lose situation.

You are the common denominator in all areas of your life, and for any part of your life to improve, you need to give yourself the attention, time, and love you deserve. Work/life balance may be an outdated model, but having a different kind of balance—inner balance—can help you manage all the ups and downs of work and life. This comes from knowing *who you are*, knowing what matters to you, and taking care of your mind and body so you can be your best self in all areas. In order to reach your potential, you need to make yourself a priority. If making yourself a priority is a challenge for you, think back to your reflection exercises and the values you uncovered in Chapter 1. You will likely notice each value is intricately linked to your health and well-being. For example, if family is important to you, recognize that to be there for your family, you need your health. If career advancement is important to you, recognize that you can't perform the way you'd like to if you don't have your well-being. Acknowledging that your values are dependent upon maintaining your health and well-being should help you place more importance on making yourself a priority by embracing a healthy lifestyle and self-care. If there isn't any fuel left in your tank, you are going nowhere fast.

Lifestyle audit

When was the last time you took a close look at your daily lifestyle choices and assessed whether they were helping you or hurting you? Are you still eating the same way you did 10 or 20 years ago? How often are you ordering in or going out to eat and how often are you making your own meals? Are you heavy-handed with the saltshaker? What are your drinking patterns throughout the day and evening? Are you sitting most of the day? Are you an elevator or a stairs kind of person?

If you want to improve your lifestyle, the first step is to take a close and loving look at where you are currently at. When you do this, be honest with yourself and make an assessment free of filters and free of shame. Begin building self-awareness around your habits and lifestyle choices, including your diet, sleep schedule, and exercise patterns, from a place of self-compassion. It can be all too easy to fall into a trap of self-judgment and frustration, which will just move you in the wrong direction. Also, avoid the comparison game. No matter how perfect someone may look to you from the outside, everyone has struggles and things they are working to improve. Doing this lifestyle audit is all about taking steps in the direction of progress and growth specific to you, bit by bit. Even little adjustments can have a big impact when made repeatedly over time.

LIFESTYLE REFLECTION ACTIVITY

Sit in a quiet space where you can relax and you won't be disturbed. Take out a piece of paper or a notebook and take a moment to reflect on how you think you are doing with your nutrition, sleep, exercise, alcohol consumption, and unhealthy habits like smoking. Rank each on a scale of 1–10, with "1" being poor and "10" being great. Think about whether there are certain times of the day, days of the week, or different seasons when you do really well in a category. Are there trends for when you struggle more in these areas? Use this as a guide to determine where you need to focus more time and energy to make positive changes that will benefit your health, your remote work productivity, and your life. If there is an area that you are struggling in and you need support, there are many helpful resources. Talk to your healthcare provider to gain insight into what is best for you.

NUTRITION—rank from 1–10
SLEEP—rank from 1–10
EXERCISE—rank from 1–10
ALCOHOL—rank from 1–10
CAFFEINE—rank from 1–10
SMOKING/OTHER—rank from 1–10
PREVENTATIVE CARE—rank from 1–10

Love what you eat and how it makes you feel

When I was practicing as a physician assistant in integrative psychiatry, one of the first things I would talk to my patients about was nutrition. I can't count how many times I got a look of surprise when I explained that what we eat impacts our *mental* health. I am sure you have heard about the importance of nutrition for your physical health, including aspects like maintaining a healthy weight, heart health, and preventing chronic illnesses, but you might not have heard that a balanced diet can also support a healthy mood and optimal performance. A sometimes surprising tidbit to help you understand the relationship between our gut health and our mental health is that about 95% of serotonin, what I like to call our "happy" neurotransmitter, is actually provided by the gut,[1] and about 70% of our immune system is actually located in our gut.[2] The exciting thing here is that just by making your nutrition a priority, there is potential for significant improvements in your overall well-being. I saw numerous people improve attention, focus, and mental well-being after reducing inflammatory foods and increasing the number of whole foods and anti-inflammatory healthy meals they consumed.

Years ago, I was sitting in my office waiting for my next patient to walk in. The man I was about to see had been in my office not too long before and we had discussed making some adjustments to his diet and doing a protocol to support a healthy gut to address some of his concerns around his focus. When he stepped into my office, he had a huge smile on his face and he seemed exceptionally excited. He said loudly, "It worked," and proceeded to tell me about his surprise and delight with the positive changes he had experienced since our last visit. I left work that day with a smile on my face, truly excited about the possibilities for people when it came to nutrition and gut health.

THE SNEAKY SNACKING TRAP

A nibble of pound cake here, a bite of a cookie there . . . Do you ever find yourself snacking more while working remotely? Maybe it's casually grabbing a handful of chips as you walk past your pantry, or mindlessly munching on a candy bar while staring at your computer screen. Without awareness, mindless snacking on inflammatory foods can become all too easy while working from home. Before you know it, that mid-morning handful of candy or bag of chips could become the norm. While working remotely can present a unique challenge in this arena, giving you greater access to more snacks and temptations, it also presents a wonderful opportunity. Unlike working in a large communal office where you may not have a refrigerator or easy access to nourishing food choices, you are in the driver's seat when it comes to what groceries you choose to have in your home, and you have ample room to store them.

To set yourself up for success here, you need to be prepared. The best time to make optimal choices when it comes to nutrition is not when you are hungrily searching for a snack. If you have ever gone grocery shopping at lunchtime on an empty stomach, you probably came home with more splurges than you normally would. If you are ravenous, it is way too easy to grab whatever looks good, regardless of whether it helps or hurts you. If you want to set the stage for making great food choices, you need to have the more nutritious options accessible and easily grabbable. You can 100% start enjoying nutritious snacks and meals amid your remote workday with some effort, intention, and planning on your end.

Some common excuses I've heard when it comes to not being able to eat healthy include "I don't have time," "Healthy food doesn't taste good," or "I don't know what I'm supposed to be eating." It can also be incredibly overwhelming if you start searching for different diets online. I have heard about and seen a wide variety of diets and lifestyle choices from my time practicing in healthcare. Some were extreme, some very restrictive, and others didn't sound enjoyable at all. I have also tried a variety of dietary lifestyles myself, from being pescetarian, vegetarian, and even trying to go vegan. While searching for the "perfect" diet, I realized that eating healthfully is not about being perfect. My current philosophy when it comes to nutrition is to not overcomplicate things. A simple rule I try to follow, which I believe everyone can benefit from, is to minimize processed foods and to increase whole foods. When you are looking to incorporate positive dietary changes, you also want your choices to be sustainable. You should enjoy the food you eat and be excited about it while making choices that will give you the nourishment and energy you deserve.

I was able to discuss lifestyle, diet, and the blue zones (the places in the world with the healthiest, longest-living populations) with Dan Buettner, originator of the blue zones concept and the host of the Netflix series *Live to 100*, on my Live Greatly podcast. Here is something that Dan shared on my show. "A few things you see in all blue zones, they're eating mostly a whole-food, plant-based diet, which means beans, nuts, greens, tubers, and whole grains. They eat meat, but only five times per month, maybe fish a couple times a week."

During my fellowship in integrative medicine, I learned a lot about the Mediterranean diet and the anti-inflammatory diet, both of which are really more of a way of living. They limit processed foods, fried foods, and added sugar, and they focus on incorporating vegetables, fruits, beans, whole grains, healthy fats, nuts, and nutritious herbs and spices.

When it comes to nutrition and how your body responds to certain foods, you are unique, which means that your nutritional needs and potential restrictions are unique. It is important to get to know your body, how it feels and how it responds to what you put into it. Do you feel sluggish after you eat lunch? Do you have digestive troubles after certain meals? This is your body giving you feedback on how it is responding to what you are putting into it. If you need help in navigating your diet, make sure to seek support from your healthcare provider and/or a nutritionist.

While I was talking with Dr. William Li, *New York Times* bestselling author of *Eat to Beat Disease*, he shared that when thinking about nutrition, people should ask themselves the question, "What can I eat to *really live*?" He went on to say that living means really enjoying your life, so you should "love your food to love your health." There are many delicious and healthy foods that will resonate with you and bring you joy to eat. You 100% do not have to be miserable to be healthy.[3]

Checkpoint

What story are you telling yourself right now about your dietary choices? Is it helping you or is it hurting you? How can you shift your story around food so that it is more empowering for you?

When you are looking to make positive changes to your diet, it can be helpful to start small and build from there. You can begin by looking at what you snack on throughout the day and then aim to make some adjustments to help support optimal health and energy. Some go-to snacks that I like to have around the kitchen include a variety of pre-cut vegetables like broccoli, cauliflower, carrots, or cucumbers to enjoy with hummus or a nutritious dip. Other choices include fresh apples to enjoy with a nut butter, a bean salad, or some tabbouleh. After you have added in some nutritious snacks, start to look at what your typical meals entail. Consider swapping out bacon or sausage in the morning for some sliced cucumbers, steel cut oatmeal, or fresh fruit. See if you can add more greens and a healthy protein to your lunch. Look to incorporate more vegetables and beans into your dinners. If possible, try to buy organic produce to minimize pesticide exposure. If that is not possible, you can educate yourself on the produce most heavily sprayed with pesticides by looking at the Environmental Working Group's Dirty Dozen and Clean Fifteen lists which show which non-organic fruits and vegetables tend to have the most and least pesticide usage. Some items on the Dirty Dozen 2023 list[4] included strawberries, spinach, apples, pears, peaches, blueberries, kale, bell and hot peppers, cherries, and green beans. Some items on the 2023 Clean Fifteen list[5] included onions, pineapple, avocados, sweet corn, cabbage, asparagus, honeydew melon, mangoes, sweet potatoes, carrots, and watermelon.

Calm mind, quality sleep

I remember how sleep-deprived I was when my kids were newborns: the nightly feedings that sometimes led to a persistent brain fog that lasted throughout the day. You probably have experienced times in your life when getting high-quality sleep seemed impossible. Maybe you're going through that right now. What I've learned (and I wish I'd known when my kids were babies) is that even when it's tough, there are some strategies you can use to help you sleep better no matter what is going on.

A common problem people face when trying to fall asleep is an over-active mind. This isn't surprising considering all the stresses from the day that bleed into our post-workday brain. I have talked with many individuals who struggle with turning off all the worries of the day when it's time to go to bed, as if their pillow has a big sign on it that says START WORRYING. If you aren't effectively managing stress throughout your hybrid or remote workday, unfortunately you may find that bedtime becomes the time to think about all the things that have gone wrong or could go wrong. On top of carrying the worries of the workday into your bedroom, your relationship with technology can set you up for a restless night's sleep. Many of us are deeply connected to our phones and tablets throughout the day and night. You may even find yourself on your laptop or your phone right up until you turn off the lights to attempt to go to sleep. On top of phones and computers, you may be watching stimulating and intense shows in the evening right before bedtime. Instead of helping our bodies, minds, and nervous systems prepare for restful sleep, these pastimes can activate our sympathetic nervous system, making us feel alert and edgy. While I am definitely a user of technology, and I enjoy a great TV series as much as anyone, there is a time and a place for it. Scrolling your phone, checking work emails, and watching thrillers right before bed will not set you up for a great night's sleep.

While I was chatting on my podcast with ABC News anchor Diane Macedo about her struggles with insomnia and the findings from her research for her book *The Sleep Fix*, she shared: "I think the golden rule for sleep in general is: if you are awake in bed long enough to feel frustrated and you don't have an immediate way to alleviate that frustration, get out of bed, do something calming and relaxing, and go back to bed when you feel sleepy again."[6] What you don't want to do is get into a pattern where your bedtime becomes your time to overthink instead of your time to sleep.

So how can you set yourself up for a great night's sleep? Establishing a healthy evening and bedtime routine has the potential to be incredibly helpful. Things like regular mealtimes and not eating dinner right before you go to sleep, having a cool bedroom, avoiding screens two hours before bed, and getting exposure to natural bright light in the morning and dim light in the evening can support your body's natural sleep rhythm. Improving the quality of your sleep can make you happier and healthier, and it can significantly improve your work performance. Building new habits takes time and repetition, so start with small changes and be consistent. Over time, you'll build momentum, and a good night's rest can become your new normal.

One challenge of working from home is that there's no way to truly "leave the office." This can magnify sleep disturbances, so it's vital that you set up a peaceful sleeping environment and keep your bedroom for sleeping, not for working. One remedy I've found helpful is to clear my mind before going to bed by making a list of any lingering "to-dos" still whirling through my brain. This creates freedom to relax and rest in the knowledge that everything I need to remember is captured on that list and ready for my attention in the morning.

Some other strategies to support restful sleep include meditation, mindful breathing, or a soothing ritual before bed to calm your mind, so you can fall asleep peacefully and wake up refreshed and energized for the day ahead. Overly stressing about needing to get a good night's sleep or aiming to have a perfect routine may actually negatively impact your ability to relax and let go for high-quality sleep. It is important not to put too much pressure on yourself here. Everyone will have a rough night's sleep once in a while, but if you find yourself struggling with your sleep or having repeated restless nights, talk to your healthcare provider to help you evaluate the cause and come up with a solution, so you get the rest your body and mind so desperately need.

Sweat it out

As a mother of two children, it's fair to say that many mornings in my life have not gone as planned. Whether it's waking up to dog puke on the floor, my kids going at a snail's pace to get ready for school, or taking an eager sip of my coffee only to realize that I'd topped it off with spoiled milk, some mornings have been stressful. On those challenging days, I have successfully relied on exercise to get myself and my day back on track. But it hasn't always been easy to find the time for it. As a remote or hybrid worker and human being, you may feel like life is sending you umpteen reasons why you can't make time to care for yourself. I mean, if you think you have to choose between wiping up the dog's puke or hopping on the Peloton, what's it going to be?

To combat these twists and turns that life throws at you, you need to make movement a top priority in your life. Recognize that when you spend time exercising, you are helping not only yourself but your family and your work as well. Since exercise can improve your health, your mood, and your work performance, everyone wins. One common challenge people face when they are looking to crank up their exercise routine is that the effort and action are not sustainable, and they drop off after a few weeks. I was invited into the United Center, the home of the Chicago Bulls and Blackhawks, to record an episode of my Live Greatly podcast with their fitness director, Jeff Powell. While talking about employee wellness with Jeff, he shared: "Start small and then you can build from there. It's about finding what works for you. Everybody's journey is different. Your wellness journey is not gonna be the same as what you see on social media."

So how can you set yourself up for making adjustments that you will actually be able to stick with and build from? Some key things to help with this include setting initial goals that you know you can accomplish and aiming to do things that you enjoy and find fun. If you hate running and you set yourself a goal of running two miles five times a week, how likely do you think it is that that exercise schedule will actually hold up? My guess is that it would be highly unlikely to last longer than a month, let alone a year or more. You would *maybe* make it through the first week and then you would probably come up with reasons to skip it because the bottom line is, you just don't enjoy it. The problem here is not that you are lazy or unmotivated, it is that running five times a week is just not the right exercise goal for you. However, if you enjoy walking and you set a goal of walking one or two miles four times a week, that would be much more approachable and much more likely to be in place in a year or two.

Another way to increase the likelihood of success is to talk to your loved ones, friends, and coworkers about your movement goals. Get support from friends and family to keep you on track. Consider working out with a friend or coworker for accountability. When you are working remotely, you most likely have the flexibility to squeeze in a 20- or 30-minute workout in your living room between work calls. You even have easy access to your closet for a quick wardrobe change. If 20 minutes is too long, schedule in 3–4 minutes of core work or stretching before you hop onto your first video call of the day, and aim to incorporate more small bursts of activity throughout the workday. If you have little ones at home with you, try to exercise before they get up, during nap time, and hey, if you need to put on a show and plop them in front of the TV for 20 minutes so you can get moving, do it. And don't feel guilty about it!

If you need even more reasons to start making regular movement a priority, one big one is that exercise has been found to be helpful in treating depression and in supporting a healthy mood.[7] Research also shows that movement throughout the day can make you more productive. So set aside some time for a walk after lunch. Aim to move around for *at least* five minutes every hour. Start taking calls while on a walk outside. Maybe even investigate whether a standing desk could be beneficial for you.

To set yourself up for success with your exercise goals, see if you can get a chunk of movement in first thing in the morning. I have found that getting my run in at the start of my day allows me to reap the benefits all day long. It also minimizes the excuses that can surface if I am trying to find time later in the day to squeeze it in. If you are just not a morning person, no worries, find a time that works for you. Just make sure you do it. If you have a day or week where your schedule is overly hectic, high-intensity interval training (HIIT) can be a solid way to work out in a short amount of time. If high-intensity workouts aren't for you, how about some yoga or other calming practices? Experiment with different exercises to see what resonates and what you enjoy. Also, make sure to talk to your healthcare team about any exercise restrictions and about any specific exercises that could benefit you as an individual.

One of the clear benefits of working remotely is that you can wear leisure clothes that are conducive to exercise, so you can move your body and then be ready for a meeting in no time. I have found that by throwing on a nice top, earrings, and some red lipstick, I am camera ready in under five minutes. I can't count how many meetings I've had with CEOs while looking polished on top with my leggings and workout socks on the bottom. No one needs to know…

Endnotes

1   Appleton J. (2018) The Gut-Brain Axis: Influence of Microbiota on Mood and Mental Health. *Integrative Medicine: A Clinician's Journal*, 17(4):28–32. PMID:31043907; PMCID:PMC6469458. https://www.ncbi.nlm.nih.gov/pmc/articles/PMC6469458/

2   Cohen, S. (2021) *If you want to boost immunity, look to the gut.* https://connect.uclahealth.org/2021/03/19/want-to-boost-immunity-look-to-the-gut/

3   Li, W. (2019) *Eat To Beat Disease: The New Science of How Your Body Can Heal Itself,* New York: Grand Central Publishing.

4   Environmental Working Group (n.d.) *EWG'S SHOPPER'S GUIDE The Dirty Dozen*™. www.ewg.org/foodnews/dirty-dozen.php

5   Environmental Working Group (n.d.-a) *EWG'S SHOPPER'S GUIDE The Clean Fifteen*™. https://www.ewg.org/foodnews/clean-fifteen.php

6 Macedo, D. (2021) *The Sleep Fix: Practical, Proven and Surprising Solutions for Insomnia, Snoring, Shift Work, and More*, New York: William Morrow.

7 Harvard Health Publishing (2021) *Exercise is an all-natural treatment to fight depression.* https://www.health.harvard.edu/mind-and-mood/exercise-is-an-all-natural-treatment-to-fight-depression.

CHAPTER 4

Time for a dance break

● ● ●

Life comes at you fast. Remote and hybrid workers know this all too well. There are always a million things demanding your attention, from dirty dishes in the sink to your growing workload and the ping of your email inbox. There is the desire to be present and supportive for your friends and family as well as the need to juggle the unexpected things that will inevitably pop up amid your workday. Then throw in the silent pull of your to-do list telling you, just send one more email, check off one more thing, before you take that break. Often, that one more thing can turn into doing two, three, or more things and before you know it, you end up not taking that break after all.

When your home and your workspace are under the same roof there are bound to be some unique challenges and stress points that you will need to overcome. Many remote and hybrid workers struggle with being unable to really unplug to shift into "home" mode at the end of the workday. When your workspace is constantly available to you, it can be all too easy to find yourself working even more hours as a remote worker.

> ### Checkpoint
>
> With all the things that you have on your plate, are you putting your own needs on the back burner?

When I was talking on my podcast with Susan MacKenty Brady, the founding CEO of the Simmons University Institute for Inclusive Leadership, she shared: "There's no scoreboard at the end of life where you get extra points or extra credit for being needless and wantless, and so what I want to be reminding everyone, and I'm practicing it myself, is: don't leave yourself behind on your own leadership journey. Don't leave yourself behind on your own life journey."

If you have fallen into a pattern of setting aside your needs and wants, or if you have developed some unhelpful or unsustainable work patterns, you are definitely not alone. The great news is that once you become aware of this, you have the power to make new choices to shift your path in a more positive direction.

While hybrid and remote work can lead to their fair share of challenges, they also present you with some incredible opportunities. When you work remotely you have more autonomy to take ownership over your health and happiness. However, to gain all the benefits of remote work, you need to be intentional with how you spend your time.

> ### Checkpoint
>
> Are you maximizing the flexibility benefits that remote work offers?

Want to schedule in a power yoga session midafternoon or grab coffee or take a walk with a friend midmorning? In the old model of work, this may have been unrealistic, but with the flexibility that remote work offers, these things are now regularly within your grasp. Being a remote or hybrid worker means that you get to incorporate stress-management techniques and self-care on your own terms, in your own way.

If you have worked in an office setting, the thought of pulling out your yoga mat in the communal office and starting to do some downward dog poses and cat-cow stretches would probably make you cringe and/or chuckle. The great news is that when you work from home you can incorporate your personal stress-reducing and health-boosting activities without having to worry about anyone staring at you strangely or judging you. Now even if adding in more stress-busting, mood-boosting activities sounds really appealing, it can be all too easy to throw breaks aside and fall into old unhelpful patterns when work and life get busy. The key here is that you need to *choose* to be more intentional with taking breaks. To help yourself do this consistently, make sure that you enjoy what you choose to do during your break time. If you hate yoga and are trying to make that your stress-busting activity, you will end up making excuses and will likely convince yourself that work is just too busy to pull away. Choose activities that you feel good about, things that you look forward to. When you notice that you are not as excited about a specific break time activity, it is time to switch it up.

Break time and fun time need to be incorporated into your workday schedule just like your meetings and calls.

For the majority of us, our boss is not going to incorporate mandatory breaks into our schedule. At the end of the day, you are the one that needs to prioritize taking regular scheduled breaks for yourself.

Checkpoint

Are you scheduling breaks and fun into your workday?

So, what are you waiting for? You can start taking ownership over your days and over your life right here, right now. Once you start using your time more intentionally, you will begin heading in the direction of more energy, vitality, and work/life harmony. Whether you are dealing with a Zoom call gone haywire, a sick child, or just trying to keep up with it all, incorporating stress-management techniques into your everyday routine will help you boost your performance and feel more psychologically stable to be able to handle whatever comes your way.

Set yourself up for a great day

Think back to when you woke up this morning. How did you feel for the first 20–30 minutes of your day? Were you stressed about the day ahead or did you feel relaxed and at ease? Were you excited and eager, or were you just kind of blah? On days when I have woken up feeling stressed or overwhelmed, it sometimes has gone a bit like this . . .

I wake up at 6 a.m. to my alarm pinging and I groggily get out of bed to grab my phone and turn off the alarm. My husband and I were up later than normal the night before watching a TV series that we had gotten sucked into, and I can feel it. I wish I had gone to bed a bit earlier. As I hit the "off" button to my alarm, I notice a news notification on my phone with an upsetting headline that makes me feel unsettled and a bit fearful. I start to check my email inbox on my phone as I walk into the bathroom, and the email that I was hoping for isn't there. A twinge of disappointment hits me. Then I notice an email from a guest I was hoping to have on my show letting me know that they aren't available. I feel a bit more bummed. Then I read another email with some requests that I am not too excited about, which I know will take me some time, and a sense of overwhelm starts to creep in. Now, before I have even brushed my teeth and walked out of the bathroom, I am already feeling annoyed and disappointed. Then, as I walk into the kitchen, I notice some dirty dishes in the sink left over from a late family dinner the night before. I go to let the dogs outside and I see that our youngest dog has left us an unwanted present all over the floor. After I clean that up, I think about all the things I need to do to get the kids off to school on time, like making lunches, and my to-do list builds. I start feeling stressed and even more overwhelmed. I head towards our sunroom, where I like to meditate in the mornings, and I sit down, trying to relax and regroup, but I feel too distracted with all the things I need to get done. After a few minutes I decide that I want to start tackling the different tasks on my growing checklist, so I head back into the kitchen.

So, where do you think I went wrong in that scenario? Was it looking at the news headline when I turned my alarm off? Was it the fact that I had stayed up later the night before? Was it checking my email inbox first thing?

Was it not taking more time for myself to try to get back on track? There were a handful of things I could have done differently to set myself up for a better morning and a better day ahead, but the main thing that went wrong here was, *I did not take ownership over my day.* I allowed the start of my day to be impacted by external forces making me feel reactive before I could even get my footing for how I wanted to show up for the day ahead.

Now let's look at what a morning where I wake up feeling invigorated, happy, and at ease looks like . . . I wake up at 6 a.m. to my alarm pinging and I step out of bed, feeling rested as I take a big stretch, and I start to think about the things that I am excited for with the day ahead. I express my gratitude with a quick internal prayer, thankful for my family, my health, and this new day as I walk over to my phone to turn off my alarm. I head to the bathroom to brush my teeth and then I walk out of our bedroom to let our dogs outside before heading into our sunroom. I get comfortable and sit for 10 minutes meditating and setting intentions for the day ahead. I do a few yoga poses and then come out to the kitchen to make my coffee and breakfast before the kids get up. I then handle making lunches and helping the kids get ready for school. Once they are off for the day, I check my emails and gain clarity on what I want to do and what I need to do for my workday ahead. I then head outdoors for a run and when I return, I feel excited and invigorated, ready to jump into work mode.

Now in this scenario, there were a few minor tweaks which had a significant impact. Instead of being reactive to what was happening around me, I got into the driver's seat and took control over my day, and you can too.

The little things in our work/life, the little habits, make a huge difference in how we feel and how we show up.

Creating your ideal morning

If you could create your ideal morning, what would it look like? If you envisioned waking up in an overwater bungalow in Bora Bora and walking out to views of a sparkling blue ocean to enjoy the sunrise while sipping on a cup of coffee before having a wonderful day ahead with your loved ones, I am right there with you . . . Now vacations aside, take a moment to think about what a great morning would look like on a workday when you wake up in your home. What are some key components that would make it so great? What are some things in your control that would not be a part of that great morning?

I am curious, in your version of an ideal morning, did you check your phone shortly after you woke up? My guess is probably not. But how often is looking at your phone first thing a part of your typical morning? With many of us using our phones as alarm clocks, doing so is an unhelpful habit that can negatively impact your stress response. According to 2023 data[1] from Reviews.org, 88.6% of Americans reported checking their phones within 10 minutes of waking up. I get it, it can be so tempting, and this is something that I have gotten into the habit of in the past, but if you fall into the trap of checking your email, looking at news headlines, or scrolling through social media first thing, you are doing yourself a disservice and are setting yourself up to be in a reactive state throughout the day.

While researching this topic, I found a Forbes article[2] that talked about how checking your phone right after waking can disrupt your brain's natural brainwave patterns that occur when transitioning from being asleep to being awake. By looking at your phone, you may be throwing your brain into alert beta waves before your mind and body even have time to get their bearings. I think of this as equivalent to waking up to your TV blasting at full volume sharing some scary and upsetting news that just occurred. Your body and brain would be like, what in the world is happening?! So why are we so drawn to our phone in the morning? With all the different features on our phones, like the ability to easily connect with people around the world, the hope of getting a positive message or response, the pulls of social media and more, research[3] has shown that using them and checking them can become addictive. When you receive a positive message, or you get a like on your social media post, you get rewarded with a release of dopamine, a feel-good neurotransmitter that is also released from things like sex, junk food, and having optimal social encounters.[4] Since you were rewarded for this behavior, you will want to feel like that again, and this is something that many marketers try to take advantage of. If you aren't aware and intentional, you may end up seeking out that feeling again and again and again, to the detriment of your attention, happiness, relationships, and health.

Checkpoint

Who is in the driver's seat with how you use your time, and where you focus your attention: you or your cell phone?

So, how can you make it easier to avoid checking your phone in the early morning so that you have space to do things that are really good for your mind and body? If you would like to continue to use your phone as an alarm clock, you could set a clear intention for yourself of not checking your phone until a certain time, and get your family involved too. Then plan enjoyable things for yourself first thing after waking up. The Forbes article[5] I mentioned earlier offered an interesting suggestion to turn your phone to airplane mode during the night and early morning. I tried it and it worked for me. I kept my phone on airplane mode until I was ready to get into work mode for the day. If you want to make it easier on yourself, or if using your phone as an alarm clock makes it too difficult to avoid scrolling, you could get a traditional alarm clock and have your phone outside of the bedroom. You could then just power off your phone at bedtime and keep it off until you have had time to get your footing for the day ahead.

Checkpoint

What are some things you can do to develop a better relationship with how you use your phone?

When you take time for yourself first thing in the morning, you are setting yourself up to successfully manage stress and feel your best. Aim to take 20–30 minutes for self-care when you wake up. Meditate, practice yoga, exercise, journal, or do something else that resonates with you and helps you prepare for the day. Embrace morning sunlight. Research[6] shows that being exposed to light in the morning is good for your internal clock and circadian rhythm. It can also help you feel more alert, and it can help you fall asleep more easily at bedtime too. Remember to drink water to hydrate and have a nourishing breakfast. By adding these healthy habits in the morning, you will face the day feeling more grounded and less reactive, which can improve your energy, productivity, and overall well-being.

Seven-day phone challenge

Set a goal for yourself of not checking your phone within at least 20 minutes of waking up. Do this for one week and see how you feel. My guess is you will feel happier and more in control of your day. Once you notice the benefits, it will be easier to stick with this for the long term. Try it and see for yourself.

Morning routines are important, but they are only a piece of the puzzle when it comes to stress management and work/life well-being. Self-care is not something you should be reserving for quiet time in the morning; it needs to be integrated into your daily routine. Taking regular scheduled breaks can help keep stress in check before it builds and starts causing problems. If you notice that you are feeling tense or anxious during the day, your body is talking to you. It is asking you to take a moment to intervene to reboot and calm down your nervous system. This is where you can insert microbreaks.

Microbreaks

Are you feeling overworked? Digital overload and Zoom fatigue are common problems while working remotely.

Staring at a screen all day, being overloaded with virtual meetings, and not taking ample time to decompress and reset in between can leave you feeling overwhelmed and drained. If you are overscheduled or if you have a lot on your plate, it can be tempting to work straight through without taking time away, but that is the wrong approach, for many reasons.

In 2021, Microsoft released the results of a small study[7] that showed the benefits of taking breaks between back-to-back video meetings. The study measured the electrical activity of the brain by using an electroencephalogram (EEG) on 14 people who had back-to-back video meetings for two hours (four half-hour meetings back-to-back). The researchers found that beta waves, which are associated with stress, kept increasing. Beta waves also spiked with transitions from meeting to meeting, suggesting increased stress during these times. They then had these same people repeat the process but this time they had them take a 10-minute meditation break between the 30-minute meetings. The researchers found that beta-wave activity dropped and brainwave patterns during the next meeting were consistent with higher levels of engagement. The takeaway from this?

Taking breaks is not a luxury. They are a necessity for your mind and body to function optimally while working remotely.

This is great intel if you are looking to be a top performer who is also healthy and happy. Micro-self-care breaks are a big part of the puzzle when it comes to building a resilient and healthy mind and body. By taking time regularly throughout the day to calm down your nervous system, you are training yourself to always return to a state of inner calm. Research[8] also showed that microbreaks (breaks of no more than 10 minutes in this research) can boost vigor and reduce fatigue. Some of the data in this research around performance showed that microbreaks may not be as impactful for all types of performance. They only had significant effects on performance with tasks that required less cognitive demands. This data showed that the longer the break, the larger the performance boost, so when it comes to performance in general, especially for more intense tasks, longer breaks may be needed for more of a positive impact.

While I was talking with world champion and professional mountain climber Sasha DiGiulian on my podcast, she shared: "[The] mental game in climbing is a player in not only how you control your nerves but also how you read and understand the puzzle piece that is a blank cliff." While you are likely not faced with needing to climb actual cliffs throughout your workday, you will have to face your own metaphorical cliffs and obstacles that pop up. When you make your mental health and well-being a priority, you will be prepared to bring your peak performance to whatever challenge comes your way.

So, the next time you are feeling overwhelmed, recognize that your brain and body are giving you feedback, letting you know that you need to pause. For many, the default response is to try to power through. But not you. Now you know that taking a micro-self-care break might be all you need to come back re-energized and refocused, or if you have been working on an intense project, you may need to take a longer break so that your performance will be at its best when you return.

One of the biggest obstacles that I see preventing people from incorporating stress-reducing activities amid the workday is thinking that they just don't have time. Here's the thing . . . some of these microbreaks don't even necessarily need to go longer than three minutes. You can get benefits from doing a two-minute breathing exercise. You can have positive results from taking 30 seconds to pause to refocus your attention to the present moment and the intentions you set for yourself that day. The key here is consistency. What do you think would have more positive benefits, consistently taking a 3–5-minute microbreak every hour throughout your workday, or taking a 20–30-minute break once a week? My vote would be for the regular microbreaks every time.

So, what are some things you could do in those 3–5 minutes? You could do some breathing exercises, take a trip to Hawaii using your mind with guided imagery (pina colada anyone?), or move your body with some yoga. You could listen to some uplifting music, journal a bit, look out a window, call a friend, or pet your dog or cat if you have one. Just do something that makes you feel good that is *not* work related.

While talking on my podcast with Lee Holden, an expert in Qi Gong (a mind/body practice rooted in traditional Chinese medicine), he shared: "If you want health and longevity, you need to move your body in strategic ways. Movement is key. So, when we're sitting at work, we can do movements in our chair, and the first place I like to start is checking in with our breathing because breath is life." Let's look at some relaxation practices that can be great ways to support you at work and in life.

Breathe

You have probably heard parents say things like "take a deep breath" while talking to an upset child. You may have even said something similar to yourself or to others during times of stress. We innately know that our breath is tied to our feelings and emotions. Your breath is a powerful tool that is always with you. It has the power to activate your parasympathetic nervous system, inducing relaxation and promoting focus.[9] Deep breathing can positively improve your mood and your stress response, shown through changes in heart rate and cortisol levels, which elevate under stress.[10] In case you haven't heard of cortisol, it is known as the stress hormone, and when you are exposed to too much for too long, it can weaken your immune system and increase your risk of anxiety, depression, heart disease, insomnia, weight gain, poor memory, digestive troubles, and more.[11]

DIAPHRAGMATIC BREATHING

This type of breathing, otherwise known as belly breathing, can help you center yourself and maintain your calm. It is breathing with your abdomen, instead of shallowly with your chest. This type of breathing can be done as a formal practice while laying down, or it can be used amid stressful moments in your day as well.

Here's how to do it:[12]

1. Comfortably lie on your back or sit in a chair with your knees bent.

2. Put one hand on your chest and the other hand on your belly.

3. Breathe in through your nose and feel your belly expand, moving the hand on your belly while you inhale. The hand on your chest should remain relatively still.

4. Exhale through pursed lips and feel your belly pull in while you exhale.

The great thing about diaphragmatic breathing is you can even use this while having conversations with colleagues or clients without anyone knowing. This one was a game changer for me when I was working with patients in high-stress environments. If I was listening to a difficult story from a patient or talking with someone who was getting worked up or reactive, I was able to stay grounded and present by using belly breathing. It can also be really helpful if you are trying to stay calm and collected while having difficult conversations with your kids or loved ones.

SQUARE BREATHING

Square breathing, otherwise known as box breathing, is another great breathing technique to add to your stress-busting tool kit. Here's how to do it:

1. Exhale all the air out of your mouth.
2. Inhale through your nose for the count of four.
3. Hold your breath for the count of four.
4. Exhale from your mouth for the count of four.
5. Hold your breath for the count of four.
6. Repeat the process four times.

4-7-8 BREATH

During my integrative medicine fellowship, I learned this breathing exercise from the founder and director, Dr. Andrew Weil. Here is how you do it:

1. Exhale all the air out of your mouth.

2. Inhale through your nose for the count of four.

3. Hold your breath to the count of seven.

4. Exhale forcefully from your mouth for the count of eight, making a whooshing sound.

5. Repeat this exercise four times.

The more that you are able to incorporate conscious breathing into your work/life, the more you can train your body and nervous system to have a healthy and more positive response to stress.

54321 EXERCISE

If you find yourself worrying or feeling stressed about "what if" scenarios, this mindfulness practice can help bring you back to the present moment.

1. Notice five things you *see*.

2. Notice four things you *feel*.

3. Notice three things you *hear*.

4. Notice two things you *smell*.

5. Notice one thing you *taste*.

Guided imagery

What if I told you that you could take a vacation without ever leaving your at-home workspace? Your mind is a powerful tool, and with guided imagery, your body can respond like it is really happening. Don't believe me? Let's try a quick exercise that I was taught during my integrative medicine training.

Visualize a big yellow lemon. You pick it up and feel the pores of the lemon in your palm. You slice a piece, slowly cutting into the thick skin, and the zippy citrus scent wafts up to your nose. You pick up a thick, juicy piece and bring it to your mouth. You suck on the lemon slice. The tangy sour juice hits the roof of your mouth. Now, did you notice that your mouth started to salivate?

For relaxation purposes, pick a time when it is safe to close your eyes and then pick a place that brings you peace and joy. It could be a stunning beach with crystal-clear blue waters, a vibrant green forest, or a spot that is unique and special to you. Visualize that place and utilize all your senses to bring the experience to life. What do you see, what do you hear, what do you smell, what do you feel, what do you taste? Spend some time in this place and when you open your eyes, enjoy feeing rejuvenated and refreshed.

Progressive muscle relaxation

This is a practice with some similarities to a body scan but in this case you will be clenching a muscle or body part and then relaxing it. Do not tense or clench a body part if you feel pain, and talk to your healthcare provider if you have any conditions that leave you unsure whether this is right for you.

Here's one way you can try this:

1. Start by clenching your forehead for a few moments and then relax it. Make sure you keep your breathing relaxed

throughout this process and check in with yourself to make sure you are not holding your breath.

2. Continue tensing and then relaxing different muscles, moving down your body until you reach your toes.

Shake it out

When I first tried the practice of Qi Gong, one exercise that was recommended was shaking. It involves gently bouncing and shaking your body, and moving and shaking your arms, hands and legs. When I tried this for the first time, I quickly realized that I felt more relaxed and invigorated afterwards. I then started incorporating this simple yet effective practice into my workday. Back when I was practicing in healthcare, I would do this shaking exercise for about 15–30 seconds in between patients to reset. There is something to the phrase "shake it off" after all.

Embrace silence

Life is likely busier and noisier now than ever before and many of us have become accustomed to having constant stimulation. With all the things coming your way, you may be dealing with information overload. One way to counter this is to intentionally incorporate moments of silence without giving in to the feeling that you have to fill those moments with activity or noise.

While I was talking on my podcast with Justin Zorn, co-author of *Golden: The Power of Silence in a World of Noise*, he shared: "We tend to think that stress, these states of dopamine-rich contraction and exertion, are what we're going for, but there also exists a more profound and expansive kind of well-being that is more linked to *silence*."[13]

Leave the guilt behind

As you begin to prioritize taking more time for your mind and body amid your workday, recognize that there are going to be times where things don't work out as planned. You might fall off track or skip the scheduled break you had set aside. You may have unexpected time-sensitive personal or professional things pop up. Don't let that deter you. This is not about perfection, it is about progress.

Checkpoint

Are you feeling guilty taking time for yourself? What are some ways you can be kinder to yourself?

While working remotely, remember that you are in charge of your well-being. Take this opportunity to look at your schedule and see where you can incorporate regular breaks into your remote workday. Add them to your calendar. If you are a manager or leading a team, make regular breaks between meetings a priority for you and your team. While talking on my podcast with Jon Acuff, the author of *Soundtracks*[14] and *All It Takes Is a Goal*[15], he shared: "The way I define potential, it's the gap between your vision and your reality. So, here's the vision of how I want my life to be. I want to be this type of mom, or I want to have this type of business, or I want to be this type of athlete, whatever. And then here is my current reality. And the space between that is your potential. And life gets really fun when you start to close that gap."

So, what can you do to start moving in the direction of closing that gap? Begin experimenting with different techniques to find what works for you, and don't be surprised when your friends and family start asking you what you've been doing because you seem so happy.

Endnotes

1 Kerai, A. (2023) *Cell Phone Usage Statistics: Mornings Are for Notifications.* https://www.reviews.org/mobile/cell-phone-addiction/

2 Rai, J. (2021) *Why You Should Stop Checking Your Phone In The Morning (And What To Do Instead).* https://www.forbes.com/sites/forbescoachescouncil/2021/04/02/why-you-should-stop-checking-your-phone-in-the-morning-and-what-to-do-instead/

3 Haynes, T. (2018) *Dopamine, Smartphones & You: A battle for your time.* https://sitn.hms.harvard.edu/flash/2018/dopamine-smartphones-battle-time/

4 *Ibid.*

5 Rai, J. (2021) *Why You Should Stop Checking Your Phone In The Morning (And What To Do Instead).* https://www.forbes.com/sites/forbescoachescouncil/2021/04/02/why-you-should-stop-checking-your-phone-in-the-morning-and-what-to-do-instead/

6 CDC Archive (2023) *Effects of Light on Circadian Rhythms.* https://archive.cdc.gov/#/details?url=https://www.cdc.gov/niosh/emres/longhourstraining/light.html

7 Microsoft (2021) *Research Proves Your Brain Needs Breaks.* https://www.microsoft.com/en-us/worklab/work-trend-index/brain-research?_lrsc=7fe5143e-2fc2-41ca-8c71-594ae587648f

8 Albulescu, P., Macsinga, I., Rusu, A., Sulea, C., Bodnaru, A. & Tulbure, B.T. (2022) "Give me a break!" A systematic review and meta-analysis on the efficacy of micro-breaks for increasing well-being

and performance. *PLOS ONE*, 17(8): e0272460. https://doi.org/ 10.1371/journal.pone.0272460

9 Zaccaro, A., *et al.* (2018) How Breath-Control Can Change Your Life: A Systemic Review on Psycho-Physiological Correlates of Slow Breathing. *Frontiers in Human Neuroscience*, 12: 353 https:// www.ncbi.nlm.nih.gov/pmc/articles/PMC6137615/

10 Perciavalle, V., Blandini, M., Fecarotta, P., Buscemi, A., Di Corrado, D., Bertolo, L., Fichera, F., & Coco, M. (2017) The role of deep breathing on stress. *Neurological sciences: official journal of the Italian Neurological Society and of the Italian Society of Clinical Neurophysiology,* 38(3), 451–458. https://pubmed.ncbi.nlm.nih. gov/27995346/

11 Mayo Clinic Staff (2023) *Chronic stress puts your health at risk.* https://www.mayoclinic.org/healthy-lifestyle/stress-management/ in-depth/stress/art-20046037

12 Cleveland Clinic (2022) *Diaphragmatic breathing.* https://my. clevelandclinic.org/health/articles/9445-diaphragmatic-breathing

13 Zorn, J. & Marz, L. (2022) *Golden: The Power of Silence in a World of Noise*, New York: Harper Wave.

14 Acuff, J. (2021) *Soundtracks: The Surprising Solution to Overthinking*, Michigan: Baker Books.

15 Acuff, J. (2023) *All It Takes Is A Goal: The 3-Step Plan to Ditch Regret and Tap Into Your Massive Potential*, Michigan: Baker Books.

PART II

Fun career, fun life

CHAPTER 5

Adding the passion to your dance

● ◉ ●

Think back to the most recent wedding you attended, you know there are many different types of dancers out on a dance floor. There are the ones that are fully immersed in their dance moves, having fun and looking carefree. There are others who are shuffling around, looking awkward and uncomfortable. There are some guests that look visibly agitated and maybe a bit angry for being dragged out there. And then there are the ones that have overindulged in some way and will probably have some regrets the next morning . . . Just like people have different responses to dancing at weddings, people react differently when they hear the word "work." For many, a special type of discomfort arises. Maybe it's a vision of groggily rolling out of bed to get ready to go through the monotonous activities of the day when all you really want to do is sleep in and have the day to relax, read a book, and spend time with your friends and loved ones. Perhaps it's a feeling of annoyance as you realize that you need to face some tasks you don't enjoy. Or maybe you remember that you are scheduled to have a formal conversation with your boss, colleague, or client who gets under your skin. While these types of responses may be widely accepted as normal or just part of work, they shouldn't be the norm. You deserve more.

That's not to say there won't be things that arise at work which are uncomfortable or that you won't enjoy, because those things will happen. But when your career lights you up, that fire burns bright enough to overtake even the most tedious and frustrating of moments.

I was able to gain some great insights into living an inspired life from my conversation on my Live Greatly podcast with Bonnie St. John. Bonnie is an Olympic ski medalist and amputee, who was the first African American ever to win medals in Winter Olympic competition, taking home a silver and two bronze medals in downhill skiing at the 1984 Winter Paralympics in Innsbruck, Austria. While talking with Bonnie, she shared: "Don't strive for normal. Strive for more. Because that's in many ways easier to do." So let me ask you a question: Have you been striving for normal? Have you led yourself to believe that you don't deserve more?

If you find yourself resonating with some or all of this, believe it or not, it is possible for you to get to a place where you are excited to wake up for the workday ahead, knowing that you are making a positive impact doing something that is truly meaningful and important to you. While I was practicing in healthcare, I saw many patients who felt like they had lost their spark. Some had gotten caught up in checking all the boxes of "normal" and they had forgotten about what really got them excited. Get the degree, check. Get a job, check. Make a good income, check. Get married, check. Have kids, check. But then what?

One afternoon when I was seeing patients, I had a physician come in to see me because he was struggling with not feeling happy and fulfilled in his work and life. He had the career that he thought he wanted. He had a loving family, but he didn't feel excited or inspired in his work/life. After talking with him for a while, I learned that he had stopped doing a lot of the things that he used to enjoy because he was dedicating all his time to his work and his family. He didn't feel like he had any time to himself. I asked him what activities he used to enjoy. He thought about it for a bit and then started to list different things that he used to have fun doing which he hadn't thought about for quite a while. We discussed the possibility of him joining a social athletic team as an outlet to build community, exercise, and have fun. If you can add some fun, excitement, and newness into your personal life, that can have a positive ripple effect on how you feel and how you show up at work and in your relationships.

Take a moment and think about your dream car. Maybe it is a cherry-red Ferrari. Maybe it is a Maserati. Perhaps it is the car you are currently driving. Now, there are a lot of parts that go into making that car run at maximum capacity. There is the engine, the battery, the transmission, the brakes, and lots more. If even one of those key parts is worn down and neglected, it will negatively impact the whole car. If one of those key parts was missing, the car wouldn't be safe to drive, and it probably wouldn't even run. Obviously, you are not a car, but in order for you to be happy and fulfilled, you also need to make sure that you are not neglecting the key components that bring you joy and meaning.

Checkpoint

What is something that you loved to do 10, 15, or 20 years ago which could be fun to pick back up?

Make it matter

I have talked with many individuals with a strong passion and drive and I have noticed that this zest and fire are even more apparent with people whose careers are tied to a greater good and something they firmly believe in. An example of this is Joel Sartore, a *National Geographic* explorer, photographer, and the creator of the *National Geographic Photo Ark*,[1] which uses the power of photography to inspire people to help protect at-risk species before it's too late. When I spoke with Joel on my podcast, he shared: "I just think, man, if I can tell this species' story well enough through the Photo Ark, we of course would never doom anything else to extinction. We of course wouldn't. It's just a matter of getting the word out, so I'm very grateful to be here today telling this story and just to let people know that there is so much out there still. Most of the species I photograph can be saved, but it's really gonna take all of us kind of pushing and pulling together. We cannot be fighting with each other over politics and ideology while the world burns."

Now you may not have a job in which like Joel you are trying to save species from extinction, but you can have a meaningful impact on the world and the greater good in your own way. Having a deep meaning and purpose tied to your work is an innate motivator and it also keeps things exciting.

Checkpoint

What positive impact on the greater good does your work have on a small scale? How about on a larger scale?

Be intentional

Think back to the knowledge and discoveries you uncovered in the reflection exercise in Chapter 1. When you know what truly matters to you, you are in a better position to set goals and plans for your future. To do this, you need to have some clear intentions for yourself. These intentions and goals can point you in the right direction, but there is not always a clear and distinctive road map. Work and life can be messy. There can be unexpected twists, turns, and detours. Sometimes a road may pop up that you didn't even know existed, which can take you to a place better than you had ever envisioned for yourself. You don't have to have the path all figured out, but having set goals can help you get started to pave the way to get you to where you want to be.

While I was talking on my podcast with Alden Mills, a prior Navy SEAL platoon commander, he shared: "So many people start looking at the mountain of work they've gotta do. You know, how big the mountain is to climb. But at the end of the day, the only way you are going to climb any mountain is staying in the moment, one action, one step at a time."

Something that I have realized throughout the years is that no one truly has it all figured out. When I was a kid I used to think that adults knew everything, but when I officially became an adult and a parent, I quickly recognized that this was not the case. On my career path I have talked with many different experts in their fields, and many of them have had differing opinions and suggestions on how to approach things. If you look at medicine, protocols and recommendations are changing regularly based on new research and new information. So, if you have been waiting until you are "ready" to go after a goal or to take that next step in your career or personal life, recognize that you will probably never truly feel ready. Instead, get clear on the things that matter, trust yourself, and just begin.

Checkpoint

What is something that you have been wanting to do but you haven't started yet because you are waiting until you feel "ready"?

When you have clear intentions, you will be able to recognize when opportunities present themselves to you and you will be able to seize those moments. Without clear goals and intentions, there will be many incredible opportunities that will pass you by without you even realizing it. We are constantly exposed to an overload of information, and our brains filter out most of it because in the moment it might not seem important. Without having a clear vision or goal for your career and set intentions for your day-to-day and overall life, you might get sidetracked by other people's problems and you may very well miss a huge opportunity simply because you weren't looking for it. Have you ever been looking for something in the refrigerator and you just can't find it? You are sure it is in there somewhere, but you just can't seem to spot it while scanning the shelves? Then you ask a loved one if they know where it is and they peek in the fridge and spot it right away? It was there all along, you just didn't see it.

Now this doesn't just apply to little things like finding the ketchup in the fridge. It applies to big things too. Do you think you would miss someone walking past you in a gorilla costume? You would most likely think that's impossible, but surprisingly, you might. The power of intention is immense. In research called the Gorilla Experiment,[2] a group of people were asked to watch a video of people, some in black shirts and some in white shirts, passing a ball. They were told to silently pay attention to how many passes were made by the people in white shirts. In the middle of this video, something extremely unexpected happened: A person dressed in a gorilla costume walked across the screen, faced the camera, and thumped their chest. Now how many people participating in the experiment do you think noticed the gorilla in the video? Shockingly, only 50% of people saw the gorilla! Many were so focused on a specific task that they ended up filtering out the other stuff. If we can miss a person in a gorilla costume thumping their chest right in front of our faces because we weren't looking for it, imagine how many subtle career opportunities we miss every day . . .

While I was talking on my Live Greatly podcast with Ellen Marie Bennett, founder and CEO of culinary work-wear brand Hedley & Bennett, she shared how acting on an unexpected opportunity while working in a restaurant kitchen led to the creation of her company. "I definitely had many dream-first, details-later moments in the journey of life and I would say that the biggest one that kicked off Hedley & Bennett was when I was working at one of these spots and one of the chefs came up to me and he said, hey, there's a girl, she's gonna make us some aprons. Do you want to buy one? And he was offering me somebody else and I was like, what? And I had had this idea already for a handful of weeks. I had been thinking about our uniforms. I hated our uniforms. They were so awful." Ellen went on to say, "So, I told the chef, I blurted out, 'Chef, I have an apron company. I will make you these aprons.' And I didn't have sewers. I didn't have a plan. I literally had nothing, but I convinced him to give me this order of 40 aprons and that's literally how Hedley & Bennett began."

If you are actively thinking about ideas and goals for your career, when a door opens, you will see it and you will be able to run through it.

Career goals

To gain more clarity on your goals for your career, let's take some time for a reflection exercise. Get out a piece of paper and a pen and think about what your ultimate dream job would look like 1, 5, 10, and 20 years from now. If your dream job is what you are currently doing, that's great, but I bet there is still room for some fine-tuning. Think about your day-to-day workday and your time off work. What are you doing? How does it make you feel?

Once you have your vision for your ideal career and situation, write down at least 10 things you really enjoy, and even love, about your current job. Then, write down some pain points you are currently experiencing with your job. Are there areas where you feel unfulfilled or parts of the workday you dread?

Now, think about how those challenging areas could be viewed in a new way that is more empowering for you. It could be that by doing those seemingly menial tasks you are really developing skills that will be marketable for your next ideal role or goal. Maybe all those video meetings are helping you fine-tune your presenting skills to get more comfortable in the public eye. Maybe those tedious tasks to keep the ball moving are teaching you patience, which will benefit you in your family life. You may discover that the time you are putting into your current role is priming you for your next promotion.

After doing this exercise, open the door for some new ideas to emerge on how to approach or address these pain points. How can you approach these areas in a new way? Is any action required? Take some time to reflect on ways you can bring out the fun in your everyday work. Only you have the power to make your hybrid or remote work fun and meaningful.

While I was talking on my podcast with Robyn Benincasa, a San Diego firefighter for more than 20 years and a world champion adventure racer, she shared: "I always say to myself, I am going to keep searching until I find the thing that wakes me up at night to dream." Robyn also said that she thinks a lot of people may be waiting for their goals to just come to them, but you need to be actively searching for new goals and exploring things that spark your interest.

You need to be an active participant to keep your spark alive, burning bright.

Here are some ways that you can add more fun into your work/life.

Making work fun

- Go to a café or a new local spot to get some work done.
- Rent a beach house for a week or a month and work remotely while looking out at the water.
- Work outside if the weather permits.
- Try working while sitting on the floor on a yoga mat or on a comfy cushion.
- Set up a virtual (or in-person, if possible) coffee with colleagues.
- Take a work call while out on a walk.
- Join a local gym and listen to a work-related podcast while exercising.
- Add some aromatherapy to your workspace.
- Update your work furniture and the pictures on your wall.
- Have a fun daily calendar on your desk with inspiring words or jokes that make you laugh.
- Create monthly goals or themes with your group, colleagues, or team where you focus on different things like mindfulness, gratitude, or movement to build community and well-being.
- Go to a work-related conference in a city you would also love to explore.
- Take daily action to work towards your bigger career goals.
- Apply for that promotion you are really hoping for.
- Go to a local garden or nature preserve to brainstorm and gain inspiration for work-related creative ideas.

- Enjoy your favorite tea or healthy beverage while working.
- Listen to music while working to see if it inspires you. Research[3] has shown that emotional use of music may help with job satisfaction and performance, but background music was shown to have a negative relationship to job satisfaction. Your preferences, the type of music you listen to, and what tasks you are doing can make a difference, so experiment to see how you respond.
- Take regular work breaks to do things you really enjoy.

Adding more fun into your personal life

- Leave a kind note for a loved one in a place that they will see it mid-day.
- Give an unexpected card to someone you care about.
- Set up a lunch with a friend you have not seen in a while that you miss.
- Join a club or a group based on something you are interested in.
- Try a new workout class.
- Laugh more. Go to a comedy show.
- Learn a musical instrument.
- Take lessons to learn a new language and plan a trip to visit a country where that language is spoken.
- Let the people you love know how much you care about them just because.
- Try out a new café or restaurant for lunch.

- Get a recipe book from the library and randomly pick a new recipe to try.
- Wear a shirt that is a fun color which makes you smile.
- Plan that trip you have been thinking about.
- Explore and hike at a local nature preserve.
- Be a tourist in your town and visit some local museums.
- Pick a new sport or activity that you would like to try and sign up for a group lesson.

Endnotes

1   Sartore, J. (n.d.) *National Geographic Photo Ark.* https://www.nationalgeographic.org/society/our-programs/photo-ark/
2   Chabris, C. & Simons, D. (2010) Bet You Didn't Notice 'The Invisible Gorilla'. *NPR.* https://www.npr.org/2010/05/19/126977945/bet-you-didnt-notice-the-invisible-gorilla
3   Sanseverino, D., Caputo, A., Cortese, C.G. & Ghislieri, C. (2023) "Don't stop the music," Please: The Relationship between Music Use at Work, Satisfaction, and Performance. *Behavioral Sciences*, 13(1), 15. https://doi.org/10.3390/bs13010015

CHAPTER 6

Knowing when to leave the dance floor

* * *

Take a moment and allow yourself to imagine you're in two separate scenarios.

Scenario one: It's 5 p.m. and you're hunched over your desk in your home office. You hear your belly rumble and your mind is racing, thinking about all the emails you still need to answer. Your head aches and your shoulders feel stiff from leaning over your computer all day. You hear the ping of a new notification as you also hear the noise of your family outside your door. A pang of guilt hits you. You really wanted to spend extra time with your loved ones tonight because you know you have been working late a lot. You power through another hour of work and you finally get out of your chair to start moving your stiff body. You hear a couple cracks as your joints adjust and calibrate to being in a new position. Your head feels like it is swimming, and you feel tired and irritable as you walk out to see your family. Even though you are physically walking out of your home office, it feels like there are invisible rubber bands keeping your mind attached to your work and your desk. As you see your family, you find yourself thinking about work and everything you will need to get done when you fire up the laptop a bit later tonight. As you muster up a smile, you really wish that you could be more excited and have more energy to be with your loved ones at the end of the day. You feel they are getting the short end of the stick, and you feel bad for not being able to bring your best self to your family time.

Now picture scenario two: It's 5 p.m. and you smile as you stand up from your desk to do your favorite stretches. You breathe deeply from your belly and then sit back down to seamlessly finish the remaining tasks for the day. You hear your kids outside your office door. You laugh and pop out to give them hugs and let them know how happy you are to see them. You spend a few minutes with them and then tell them that you have a couple of things to finish before you can wrap it up for the day. You head back into your office to write your to-do list for the next day. You do one last assessment and then officially activate your out-of-the-office notification and log off. You walk out of your office and go to change your clothes to get ready for your quick walk outside to officially get into "home" mode. You feel excited and present, looking forward to all the fun the evening has to offer.

Now, I don't know about you, but if I had to choose which of those realities to live in, I would pick scenario two every single day of the week. That said, many of us unintentionally end up with something more like scenario one. I was recently talking with a friend who was feeling overwhelmed with everything she had on her plate. She felt like work got the best parts of her and then her family got the leftovers. The good news is that even if your current situation falls into that category, it does not need to be stuck there. By integrating healthy habits, rituals, and supportive boundaries into your workday, you can truly thrive while working from home. You can arrange your work/life and manage your time so that you have the energy to do everything that truly matters to you.

> ### Checkpoint
>
> Do you feel drained and depleted at the end of most workdays? On workdays where you have felt energized at the end of work, what were you doing?

Rituals for a happier you

If you have had houseguests for an extended period of time, you know the impact that getting out of your routine can have on your mental and emotional state. With people staying in your home, even when they are family or close friends, you may feel the need to be consistently "on." Maybe you miss your quiet time in the morning where you typically sit and savor your coffee, or perhaps you miss being able to watch your favorite show before bed without worrying about whether others will like it. Maybe you miss being able to walk around in your mismatched pajamas without giving it a second thought.

I was talking with a friend who had been so excited to have family friends that had moved out of state come in to visit them. While we were catching up on the phone, she was about four days into their stay. While she was really happy to see them, she was quickly realizing that the one week they had originally planned for the stay was a bit too long. She was really missing her routines and her personal time, which was leaving her feeling edgy, irritable, and tired. This really isn't surprising because there is a soothing comfort in routines. Even vacationing has the potential to be stressful if you can't continue doing some of the rituals that nourish you.

Establishing habits that stick

As human beings, we are creatures of habit. Some of those habits are extremely important and helpful, others not so much. Through my personal and clinical experience, there are five key things that I have seen as critical contributors to creating and sustaining new healthy habits. Number one: whatever you are trying to incorporate, it needs to be meaningful to you. Number two: you need to make it something that you actually want to do. If someone else is telling you to do something but it doesn't really matter to you, and if you don't enjoy it, there is an extremely slim chance that that new behavior will stick. Number three: it needs to be something approachable that you can easily incorporate into your day and life. Number four: it is helpful if it is something for which you will receive some positive reinforcement or a reward. And number five: having family, friends, a community, and an environment that support you can make a big difference.

So, how should you be going about creating new healthy habits to help you move towards work/life harmony and peak performance? Research[1] shows that connecting a new behavior to a regular external cue can support it in becoming a habit. That cue can then become the trigger for your new healthy behavior. So, get specific on where and when you are going to be adding in this new behavior. Is it at 7 a.m. during breakfast every day? Is it at 9:30 p.m. as you are winding down for bed? Is it whenever you wash your hands? Is it when you first log onto your computer each workday? When these new desired behaviors are naturally paired with times of the day and specific activities you are already doing, they are more likely to become automatic, just like putting on your seatbelt when you get into a car. But how long do you have to repeat a behavior for it to become second nature? Research[2] shows that it will get easier with time, and that with consistency you will likely have this new behavior become automatic within 10 weeks. Now what if you are trying to stop a bad habit? In this case, research[3] has shown that instead of just trying to stop this unwanted behavior, *replacing* it with a healthy behavior can actually be more effective.

Let me give you an example of what this could look like. Susie is a remote worker in her mid-40s and she has let her health and well-being slide over the past five years. As a new year approaches, she decides that she wants to lose some weight, start exercising, and stop eating so much junk food. She has tried to lose weight in the past and while the changes she made sometimes worked for a short while, the results have not been long-lasting. Susie's doctor recently told her that losing some weight could be beneficial for her health.

Now pretend that you are in a café sipping on your beverage of choice and getting some work done when you overhear Susie talking to a friend about this. In scenario one, Susie tells her friend, "Ugh. I *can't* eat junk food anymore" as she longingly glances over to the muffins in the display case. "And I *have to* start exercising to try to lose ten pounds." In scenario two, Susie tells her friend, "I am really excited about making my health a priority this year. I am starting small by *adding in* a serving of fruit every morning with my breakfast" as she smiles and looks down at her bowl of berries. "There is a new smoothie place that just opened around here. Would you be up for meeting there next time? I'm also *looking forward to* starting to walk outside for 15 minutes every morning before work at 8 a.m. Would you want to join me on my walk sometime?"

In scenario one, Susie sounds annoyed, and her goals sound forced. Her nutrition goal is focused on what she couldn't do versus what she could do. Her exercise goal is unspecific and vague. In scenario two, Susie's goals sound more like desires and they are more specific, approachable, and fun. They are also connected to specific activities (breakfast) and times of day (8 a.m. before work), which can better help them become habits. She seems to be looking to put herself in environments to promote her new desired behaviors (the new smoothie spot) and she is also looking to build community by inviting her friend to walk with her.

Between the two, Susie's approach in scenario two is much more likely to succeed. She shares clear goals, she starts with small things that can build momentum with time, and she is putting into place approachable, actionable steps which sound sustainable.

Checkpoint

What is a new, approachable healthy habit to support you in your work/life that you can tie to a daily activity you are already doing?

In addition to optimizing the language you use and the mindset you have around behaviors and goals, another way to support healthy habits is with rituals. Rituals are repeated actions that can add more meaning and depth to your life. A simple activity can be made into a meaningful ritual by having the intention of being fully present and engaged in the activity. Some common daily rituals that you can be more present for include savoring your morning coffee, telling your kids and significant other you love them before bed, or taking your dog for a walk. Rituals can also make the workday much more meaningful and enjoyable. You can turn your daily video meetings or tedious tasks you typically don't enjoy into things you might even look forward to by incorporating a ritual. Maybe you start using a warm shoulder wrap every time you need to respond to your emails. Perhaps you intentionally relax your muscles with a mini body scan right before Zoom meetings and then you incorporate relaxed diaphragmatic breathing throughout the call. Or maybe your virtual meetings are when you get to sip your favorite tea.

Any work activity can be given a makeover by incorporating rituals.

There are some key moments when rituals can play a significant role and one of these times is during transitions. When you are transitioning from remote work mode to family mode or vice versa, it can be challenging to successfully master it. Your mind needs guidance to know what to focus on and what is important. By fine-tuning your transitions you are setting intentions for what you are about to do and where your mind should be focusing its attention, whether that's creating a work presentation or playing soccer with your kids in the backyard.

Checkpoint

What is a ritual you can do to ease your transition from work to family or personal time?

Commute to your home office

With remote work, you don't have to sit in an hour of traffic to get to the office, but you do lose that built-in transition time to let your mind wander as you move from home to work mode. According to a 2023 TravelPerk survey[4] of 1,000 workers in the UK, 46% of respondents said their favorite perk of hybrid work was spending less time commuting. While there are some huge benefits here, transitions from your workday to your personal and family time are crucial for being present and engaged and for avoiding the issue many remote workers complain about: difficulty unplugging.

So why not create your own custom commute to work at home? Make a point to leave the house for a walk in the morning before work and in the evening before you "come home" and use it as your "commute" time to help clear your mind. This will help you enter your workday or your family time clear-headed and grounded. If the weather is crummy or if you don't want to take a walk, think about what you would do with your time if you were commuting to work via train or car. Would you listen to a podcast? Listen to music? Listen to a meditation app? Do a crossword puzzle? Try out some of those activities around transition times to help your mind settle down and prepare for a new space.

Back when I was practicing in healthcare, I had a man coming in to see me with a prestigious high-stress job, and he was struggling with poor focus and lack of energy. Let's call him Charles. Charles was go, go, go all the time. He would work all day and then he would be out at client dinners late into the evening, at times overindulging in food and drink.

After talking with Charles about his struggles and his habits, one suggestion I made was to start using his commute time, when he took the train, to incorporate a stress-management practice. I recommended downloading a meditation app to try a short meditation while using headphones on the train. Charles had never meditated and he was a bit skeptical about trying this out. I told him that it was really more of a relaxation exercise, so he agreed. The next time Charles came in, he expressed how he was pleasantly surprised with the improvements he had noticed since incorporating this practice. His focus and his energy were improving. The addition of this ritual was only a small piece of Charles' self-improvement journey, and he had other adjustments he needed to make to get to where he wanted to be, but this small step helped him build the momentum to continue to make tweaks and adjustments so he could feel his best in his work/life.

Dress the part

Think back to a favorite outfit that you had as a kid. How did you feel when you were wearing it? I had a black jacket with colored glass rhinestones that I absolutely loved, and I still smile when I think of it. When I got it for my birthday, I ran up to my room to try it on and then I happily strutted out to show my family, feeling a newfound sense of courage and confidence.

What we wear impacts how we feel.

Our clothing choices can influence our confidence and our mood. They can also guide our actions by helping us get into a mindset for a particular behavior. Whether it's putting on an apron when you are going to cook a meal, changing into running clothes to head to the gym, or pulling out your power outfit to wear before a big work meeting, clothing is a tool you can use to help guide your mind, your attention, and your focus. Something as simple as changing your clothes at the start of your workday and then at the end of your workday can help your mind transition to a new space. Changing clothes before and after work is common for individuals who work in an office setting, but when you work remotely, you don't always have this same need. With remote work you can easily get away with wearing loungewear all day, and if you have a video meeting, you can keep the lounge pants on and just throw on a nice top. While this can be a comfortable option, it does not do you any favors when you are looking to differentiate between work mode and home mode.

Just like superheroes have their capes and masks that they put on while they are working, having some work-specific gear can help guide your mind to be in work mode. When you are looking to shift over to family time or me time, having different gear for that is also helpful. While this can be incorporated with entire outfit changes, it can also be done in subtle ways, like putting on your favorite slippers or cozy socks after logging off work. Don't underestimate the power of these subtle changes. They can have a strong impact!

Checkpoint

What clothes make you feel the most confident and productive while working?

Use technology to help you

Are you in charge of your technology or is it in charge of you? With cell phones by our sides all day long, many of us have gotten to the point where technology has its invisible reins on us, whether it is with mindless scrolling or scattered attention from glancing at notifications, or phone checking. It takes awareness and intention to reclaim control and develop a healthy relationship with technology.

Instead of letting technology overtake your personal and family time, use it to help you. Set reminders to incorporate rituals throughout your workday and during transition times. When you have completed the necessary things for your workday, activate your away-from-the-office notification. Update your email signature letting people know your typical work hours and response times so you don't feel pressured to respond after hours. Turn off unnecessary notifications. Silence your phone. Turn technology into a supporter of your well-being and happiness instead of a deterrent.

Boundaries with work

I have talked with many different executives and when the topic of boundaries at work comes up, here are some common things that they have shared. No one is going to set boundaries for you. It is easier to put boundaries into place early rather than to try to implement them down the road. Setting boundaries can be uncomfortable. When it comes down to it, having healthy boundaries between your work and your life is incredibly important, but it is not always easy. The lines between work and life are not always drawn in permanent black marker. Sometimes they are drawn in a pen that gets smeared, a pencil that gets erased, or a crayon that is messy and looks more like a scribble.

When you are looking to create and maintain healthy boundaries in your work and life, there is not one perfect recipe, or a one-size-fits-all approach. You need to look at what you value, how you spend your time, what chapter you are on in your life, and what is most important to you. Then you need to get clear on what your non-negotiables are. This can take some trial and error and some uncomfortable moments to figure out what works best for you. And sometimes, just when you think you have it all figured out, work or life throws you a curveball. Having healthy boundaries is a continuous process that will evolve and change, but it is your job to stay on top of it, not a job for your bosses, your colleagues, your friends or your family. Wherever you are at in your boundary-setting journey, here are some things to help you, whether you are trying to establish new boundaries or trying to hold true to boundaries already in place.

Communicate, communicate, and communicate some more. Sometimes what we think is completely apparent to others is not even on their radar. If you are dealing with a challenge or struggle related to work, your boss and your team won't know what is happening if you don't tell them. There is a great example of this in the following story. After one of my talks on corporate wellness and redefining work/ life balance, where I was talking to a team of less than 100 people, many of whom worked remotely, I opened the floor up to the audience for any thoughts or questions. A woman in the audience, let's call her Sarah, hesitantly raised her hand. Sarah shared how she was really struggling to find time for self-care because her mornings and her days were so busy. She had her hands full with getting her kids off to school and then as soon as they were out the door, she was expected to be logged in on her computer for work. She didn't have time in the morning to compose herself to really feel grounded and ready for the workday. She asked me what I suggested.

After Sarah shared this, something wonderful happened. The leader of her department, who was also in the audience, spoke up and said that he had no idea that she was feeling that way, and he was happy she said something. He told her that they could be more flexible with her schedule and asked her if it would be helpful to adjust her hours so that she could log in a bit later. He asked her to connect with him first thing the next week for them to discuss options. This potential solution never would have been brought to the forefront if Sarah had not had the courage to share some of the challenges she was facing. If you have too much on your plate, if you are spread too thin, or if there are unrealistic expectations or deadlines in your workplace, most of the time things won't change until you open the lines of communication around them.

When you are discussing stress points, challenges, new boundaries, or requesting additional time off or an adjusted schedule, one way to set yourself up for a desirable outcome is to include potential solutions. Many leaders that I have spoken with appreciate it when requests have been well-thought-out and are solution-focused. For example, if you are requesting three days off during a peak work time, coming to your boss with a plan already in place for coverage while you are away will make it easier for them to say yes. If you come in demanding the time off without having set up any coverage, the conversation could go a bit differently.

If you struggle with setting boundaries, or if you categorize yourself as a people-pleaser, the following reframe around it may be helpful.

Setting boundaries is a form of self-respect.

Being able to set boundaries is actually an act of self-care and self-love. When you have boundaries in place you are showing that you value your health, your well-being, your family and your friends, as well as your career success.

While you might feel pressured to say yes to something at work that is not a top priority or something that is not in your scope of work when you have already made a personal commitment or your workload is overflowing, doing so is a disservice to yourself, your prior commitments, and your work performance. A co-worker that I worked with in the past, let's call her Erin, really struggled with saying no. She was very excited about dinner plans one evening that she had set for 7 p.m. with an old friend she hadn't seen in quite a while. Erin didn't do much outside of work, so this dinner was a big deal for her. As I was heading out at 6 p.m., I stopped into her office to tell her to have fun at her dinner and she looked upset. Our boss, let's call her Kate, had some things that had come up and Kate was expecting Erin to stay until it was all finished. Erin didn't think she was going to be able to make it to dinner after all and she was going to have to cancel. I asked her why she didn't just let Kate know that she had a personal commitment. It didn't sound like what needed to happen was urgent at all and it could easily have been handled the next day.

Erin looked stressed and said she wasn't comfortable doing that. Unfortunately, this was not a one-time occurrence for Erin. The dynamic that had been set was that she would be available absolutely whenever Kate asked anything of her, and she wouldn't leave before Kate did. While maybe not intentionally, Kate took advantage of that, encroaching on Erin's personal time and expecting her to always say yes, regardless of the hour.

You may have heard the saying: you teach people how to treat you. I think there is some truth to this phrase in certain circumstances, particularly with setting boundaries. That said, sometimes you can do everything "right" and people can still be rude or mean, etc. This is when it is important to remember that you can only control yourself.

Checkpoint

Where are you saying "yes" in your professional life when you should really be saying "no"?

Now Kate was my boss too, but interestingly I was able to uphold my personal commitments while working there. There were many times when I left the office before Kate did without an issue, and she was supportive and respectful of my time. So, what was the difference? A key difference was that there were patterns and habits that had been established between Erin and Kate that were unhelpful. There were a lack of boundaries and respect for personal time. There was also some fear and a lack of security for Erin, so that she did not feel comfortable communicating with Kate about her needs. Kate then overstepped with her requests and expectations for Erin.

If you have been in an uncomfortable situation like this before, or if you find yourself in one now, you do not need to be stuck there. You can begin right now by making setting boundaries a priority. Expect it to be uncomfortable, especially at first, but recognize that it is necessary to begin reclaiming your time and the things that you truly value.

Checkpoint

Are there certain people that you need to have healthier boundaries with? If so, how can you begin to establish them, starting today?

If you struggle in this arena, I feel you. As with other big wellness-related changes in your life, I recommend starting slow and building momentum. When I started my company, I was saying "yes" to way too many LinkedIn requests for a quick call. I was new to LinkedIn and social media in general and when a request came in, I felt pressured to comply. I didn't want to be rude and say no. In reality, I ended up wasting a lot of time and I was getting pitched to left and right. I wasn't being selective enough with who I was saying yes to or where I was focusing my attention. Even when I knew whatever was being pitched wasn't for me, when I was asked, "Can I send you more information?" I would tend to say, "Yes, sure," which would result in more emails coming into my inbox. A big shift happened for me when I realized that I needed to set healthier boundaries to protect my time, my energy, and my version of work/life harmony. I became much more selective with my "yes" responses and if I wasn't interested in something, I learned to say, "Thank you for sharing this with me, but it's not the right fit. I don't need more information, but I do wish you the best." With this came freedom. I learned my lesson, and while I'm still not perfect with this, the majority of the time now I don't say yes unless I really want to.

After giving a keynote to an audience where I shared some suggestions around creating healthy boundaries, I walked backstage and the event planner approached me. She said that the talk really resonated with her and that she found herself reflecting on the blurred boundaries between work and life for herself. Being an event planner can be hectic. She realized that she had fallen into the habit of working late into the evening on her laptop, responding to emails and doing other activities that could really wait until the next day. She decided that she was going to start leaving her laptop in her office at the end of the workday to remove the temptation of checking emails and doing work-related activities during her personal time.

Small adjustments like this work. If you don't have your laptop or your phone right in front of you, or if you don't bring them along during family outings, etc., you won't be drawn to checking them. Aim to make it as easy as you can to create and keep boundaries.

Checkpoint

What simple boundary can you create, starting today, to help support an optimal workload or schedule?

Endnotes

1   Gardner, B., Lally, P. & Wardle, J. (2012) Making health habitual: The psychology of "habit-formation" and general practice. *British Journal of General Practice,* 62(605): 664–6. doi: 10.3399/ bjgp12X659466. PMID: 23211256; PMCID: PMC3505409. https://www.ncbi.nlm.nih.gov/pmc/articles/PMC3505409/

2   *Ibid.*

3   American Heart Association (2023) *How to Break Bad Habits and Change Behaviors.* www.heart.org. https://www.heart.org/en/healthy-living/healthy-lifestyle/mental-health-and-wellbeing/how-to-break-bad-habits-and-change-behaviors

4   TravelPerk (n.d.) *Top hybrid work trend stats from companies in the UK for 2024.* https://www.travelperk.com/blog/top-hybrid-work-trend-stats-from-global-companies/

CHAPTER 7

Make your moves count

• • •

How productive do you feel in your everyday work/life? Do you regularly get into a flow with work, or do you find yourself getting easily distracted, struggling to find creativity and peak performance? Do you jump from task to task and get regularly sidetracked by the buzz of your phone, the pull of social media, or the glimpse of dirty dishes or other housework that needs to get done? Hybrid and remote work can fuel productivity in many ways, but it also can take away from it if you don't have helpful tactics in place. There are a lot of factors that go into optimizing your work performance and one powerful yet simple one is your environment. Your workspace matters, a lot.

Imagine that you're at your friend's house for an outdoor barbeque, let's call him Mark, and after enjoying a drink you head inside to search for the restroom. Mark works remotely and you know that he has been feeling stressed with his job recently. He's told you that he has been feeling overwhelmed and there is too much on his plate. Mark has also been complaining to you about feeling bored and uninspired at work, and he's said that he doesn't think he is being valued or incentivized.

While you are walking down the hall to the bathroom, you pass a room with the door open which you think is

Mark's home office. Feeling curious, you peek inside to find a rigid black chair and a fold-up brown table in the center of the room with a computer, papers, and some candy wrappers strewn across it. The walls are beige, with one picture on the wall made up of some dark and gloomy colors. There is one small window with a view of an air-conditioning unit. It smells a little stale in there and you see a trash bin under the desk that needs to be emptied. It looks like this room was thrown together at the last minute and hasn't really been thought out. You find yourself feeling kind of bad for Mark for having to work in there on a regular basis. You wonder if he would feel better about his job if he had a more inviting workspace to be in every day?

The next weekend you head over to see a different friend, let's call him Josh, who recently moved into a new house. He and his wife Julia have spent a lot of time decorating and they give you a tour. As you are walking around, you ask Josh about work and he says it's been going really well. He fills you in on his new hybrid work schedule and how he has been working remotely quite a bit more. When he starts telling you about some of the things he has been working on, you can hear the excitement in his voice. Josh tells you that when they were looking for a new home, having a great office space was really important. He then opens a door to show you his home office and as you walk in you find your-self smiling. You notice a sleek white desk with a modern, comfortable-looking chair by large windows with a view of an oak tree and purple flowers in bloom. There are a few plants scattered across the room and you notice a fresh scent of citrus, which you see is coming from a bowl of oranges on a side table. You notice some family pictures on the wall and snapshots of some great vacations Josh and Julia have told you about. As you walk out of Josh's office you find yourself thinking, now this is a place that I would want to work every day. Feeling inspired, you then start mentally planning your home office makeover…

Having a great home office is not always cut and dry, but wherever things are at for you, making some small or some big adjustments can have a significantly positive impact. While I was talking on my podcast with Luke Caldwell, designer and HGTV star, he shared: "It is important to have a space where you want to be. And so, for me, I have always approached design like songwriting. So, as a musician, you know, when you are writing a song, you are trying to create a feeling."

Checkpoint

What feeling do you want to have when you walk into your office?

As a remote worker, I have played around with working from different spots in my home to see where I could happily get the most work done in the most efficient matter. I started out working from our kitchen and then I would periodically use my husband's office when he was out for meetings or traveling for work. At times this worked okay, but I found that being in a main living space led to regular distractions and scattered attention. I could see the dishes from the corner of my eye. I knew the laundry room was right around the corner with loads of clothes waiting to be washed. I could hear the Amazon truck pulling up to our home for a delivery.

I would break up my workflow and chat with my husband every time he would enter the kitchen to grab a snack or a drink. Having my workspace in a common area in our home led to many start-and-stop moments and it was not conducive to more extended states of creativity and productivity.

Then Brian had a wonderful idea of converting our dining room to my office. We really didn't use the space as a formal dining room, especially during the COVID-19 pandemic, and having it become an office would be a much more functional usage of the space. He decorated it for me as a birthday surprise and I was so excited when I walked in to see the completed space. It looked great, and I really enjoyed having my own spot. After living and working with this office space for a while, I found myself gravitating to our sunroom to work when I wanted inspiration, or if I needed to boost creativity. There was a lot of natural light in there, with views of nature, and it was a room that I loved to be in. Over time I found that I was spending less time working in my office/our old dining room because I found that the space didn't leave me *feeling* as inspired or productive as our sunroom. I was beginning to do a lot of writing and other creative projects and I felt like I needed a space to work where I really enjoyed being. After some reflection we decided to convert my office/dining room into a workout room and to turn the corner of our sunroom into a workspace. My husband found a great convertible desk that functioned as a desk for sitting that could be easily adjusted into a standing desk. The lighting was great. There were incredible views of trees, birds, and other animals and I felt inspired and happy in the space. As I settled into my new office space, I realized that this workspace gave me the *feeling* I was searching for.

Checkpoint

Walk into your office space and notice how you feel. Are you excited, relaxed, at ease? Are you annoyed or edgy? How you feel is feedback, and it can help guide you to know where adjustments need to be made to support optimal performance.

Hacks for your home office

You don't have to remodel or spend thousands to have an uplifting and empowering remote workspace. What is something you can do, today, to introduce a better feeling into your office? One simple yet effective task that offers a big bang for its buck is eliminating clutter and having ample space for storage to keep your space tidy. Even if you don't think that clutter impacts you, test it out. Clean your workspace and then sit down to work for the day. See how you feel compared with before. I can almost guarantee that you will feel more at ease, and you will find it easier to focus on the task at hand without a mess around you.

Another element that can really impact our mood is natural light. A study[1] that looked at how daylight exposure and windows impacted office workers' health and sleep quality showed that workers with windowless environments reported poorer sleep quality and had poorer scores for role limitations due to vitality and physical problems. Office workers with more light exposure had improved sleep quality and duration, improved physical activity and quality of life. Seemingly simple things like light exposure have a big impact, influencing our circadian rhythm, mood, alertness, and more.

Aim to work in a space with windows and position your desk to a view you enjoy. Research[2] shows that viewing nature can help us relax and recover from stress, and this result can be from seeing it in its natural state or even from viewing images of nature in photos or videos. Think about all the micro-stressors that can occur during your remote or hybrid workday, and the added benefits that could be had from having access to this natural stress reducer. The perks of having windows and a view you enjoy are not just applicable to workspaces. During my integrative medicine fellowship, I learned about the impact that our environment has on healing. There has even been research[3] into how scenery may influence recovery after surgery, with a study showing that patients that had a room with a view of nature had shorter hospital stays and took fewer potent pain pills post-surgery than those who had rooms overlooking a brick wall.

Another important component of crafting your ideal workspace is paying attention to where it falls in relationship to the active living spaces in your home. Aim for a workspace separate from your living area, and if this is not possible, create an office nook or consider using a room divider, depending on your space. Choose furniture that you are excited about and a chair that is ergonomically correct. Depending on the location in your home, think about using noise-canceling headphones if you need quiet. Consider getting a whiteboard to write down your to-do list and other inspiring ideas. Let your workspace be a room that supports creativity and getting into a flow state.

Some other simple things you can do to make your home office more inviting include bringing the outdoors in with plants and flowers. Consider incorporating pleasant smells with citrus, or look into the potential benefits of aromatherapy and play around with different color choices. Research has shown that scent has the power to impact our performance and alertness, with one study[4] showing that the scent of peppermint supported recalling information and staying alert, especially when the study subjects were getting fatigued. This study showed that having the scent released intermittently on and off was more effective than having it released continuously.

Research[5] also shows that color in the workplace influences a worker's mood, performance, productivity, creativity, and well-being. But which color is best? Research[6] has shown mixed results on what the best colors are for different things, but blue and green have been consistently found to be the favorite colors, and colorful workspaces seemed to increase performance. Some research has shown that workers may prefer to work in a white environment, but there is also research showing that working in a white workspace resulted in making the most errors. Some of this data showed that blue and green workspaces were associated with a sense of well-being, with green having the most positive emotional response. The color red can be stimulating, and positive and negative effects were seen with this color. So, when you are trying to decide what colors to have in your workspace, the best question here is really, which color is best for you? See which colors resonate with you and which hues give you the feeling you are aiming for. In addition to the colors in your workspace, be selective in your artwork and choose to have pictures hanging up or on your desk that you enjoy and that help you connect to your core values. Make sure your home office has your personal touch, with meaningful pieces that bring you joy.

Checkpoint

How does the current color scheme in your workspace make you feel?

Now even if your workspace is organized and clean, if the rest of your house is messy it can be distracting. Setting up a schedule for cleaning the house, recruiting the help of other members of the household, or hiring a person to help with these household tasks can help you focus on the work at hand instead of all the things that need to get done around the house.

Your work environment is, of course, just a piece of the puzzle when it comes to productivity and performance. In addition to optimizing your work environment, successfully managing your time, focusing on high return on investment tasks, and minimizing distractions can help you have extremely productive workdays in your home office.

Time blocking

You know that feeling when you have an overwhelming amount of work to do and it just doesn't seem like there's enough time in the day? For a lot of people, the instinct is to put their nose to the grindstone to finish all the work, even at the expense of work quality and personal well-being. However, powering through your workload without taking time away from your computer or your desk can actually negatively impact your productivity. Slack's 2023 workforce index[7] based on a survey of over 10,000 desk workers showed that 50% of those surveyed said they rarely or never took breaks and unfortunately they were 1.7 times more likely to experience burnout. Those that regularly took breaks had 13% higher scores for productivity, 43% greater overall satisfaction, as well as a 43% greater ability to manage stress. Employees that felt pressured to work after hours were 20% less productive than those who could log off at the end of the workday, and they also had poorer scores for stress, burnout, and overall satisfaction. That said, those who worked outside of typical business hours by choice, for personal matters or personal scheduling preferences, did not have those negative results, and interestingly they even had a slight increase in their scores for productivity and wellness. Could that be because they were adapting their work schedule based on their unique needs, and perhaps were making time during their workday for all the things that really mattered to them?

Instead of feeding into that inner bully pushing you to do more and more, which can lead to your mind and your body revolting, experiment with new ways to work to see how you can be more efficient and more productive while actually feeling good while doing it. One way to optimize productivity is by having active work blocks mixed in with resting or regrouping blocks. The Slack research mentioned above showed that the most productive people are 1.6 times more likely to block time for specific tasks. Now there are different ways that you can incorporate time blocking. One possibility is the 52-17 model. This is where you work for 52 minutes and then take a 17-minute break away from your computer and your work.

A time-tracking app called DeskTime conducted a study[8] back in 2014 and found that the 10% most productive users were taking effective breaks. At that time, the most productive people were working for about 52 minutes followed by a 17-minute break, resulting in a work/break ratio of 52/17. DeskTime decided to repeat this study in 2021[9] and found some startling new data. The top 10% most productive people in this newer study were on average working for 112 minutes and then taking a 26-minute break, and this was not necessarily something to be proud of. In the article[10] discussing these new DeskTime findings, it was suggested that this shift could be due to overworking, since many people had started working from home. From 2014 to 2021, a lot changed. There was the COVID-19 pandemic as well as a surge in remote work. Those shifts have impacted the way that people work, how often they take breaks, and what they do on their breaks. The DeskTime article[11] discussed how with more people working remotely, breaks actually may have become longer not to do enjoyable things but to do more work around the house—putting in a load of laundry, etc. This shift from the 52/17 model to the 112/26 model may mean that many workers are moving in the wrong direction when it comes to well-being and mental health at work. Don't let yourself or members of your team be a part of that trend.

> ### Checkpoint
>
> Have you found yourself working for longer periods than you used to? Are you using your breaks to do things that you enjoy or to do different types of "work"?

Being intentional with your work and break ratio can help you maximize your productivity and optimize the rewards of your work and break time. Try out the 52/17 model and if you love it, great. If not, play around with adjusting the ratio a bit to see what works best for you. When you are taking breaks, detach from your computer and use the time to read, go for a walk, play with your kids, talk with a friend, have a healthy snack, listen to music, do a self-care activity, or participate in something you enjoy that is not work-related. While it can be tempting, make sure you are not using your break time just to get stuff done around the house, unless it is a fun project that you are excited about. Incorporate the household activities and tasks into other parts of your schedule or create a specific block just for that. If you spend your break time doing the dishes and picking up clothes from the floor, you are going to feel like you need a real break after your "break." Segmenting your work into these 52-minute blocks can be helpful in structuring your day and maintaining productivity because the work you will be doing in those 52 minutes will be higher quality than if you worked nonstop.

Overcoming procrastination

We all have found ourselves in the situation of putting something off until it absolutely has to get done. Maybe you have one month to finish a project but you don't dig into it until a week before it is due. Perhaps you have found yourself scrambling at the last minute to meet a deadline that has been on your radar all week and it needs to be in your boss's mailbox in just three hours. Or maybe you have been putting off larger projects and goals for months or maybe even years—writing a book, doing that home project, going to that fitness class you have been talking about forever. In my own life, I have found that I tend to procrastinate around things that overwhelm me, big things that are outside of my comfort zone, and things that I am just not really excited about. I also seem to procrastinate around things that I just don't want to do.

Research[12] suggests that procrastination may really be a means to try to avoid negative emotions and an attempt to regulate our moods by avoiding tasks that elicit negative responses. What this sounds like to me is that procrastination may actually be a misguided coping mechanism. In addition to this, procrastination may be tied to something called the present bias,[13] where we choose immediate gratification from a present activity versus working on something that would provide a longer-term reward in the future. There have been nights where I have looked at the dishes in the sink and thought having a cup of tea and sitting down to watch a fun TV show seems much more appealing right now. I have always regretted that choice after waking up to crusted dishes the next morning.

Deadlines can also play a role in procrastination. While you may think that having a longer amount of time to get something done could be helpful, longer deadlines may negatively impact pursuing a goal and may actually promote procrastination. Research[14] has shown something called a deadline effect, where having a longer deadline can lead people to believe that the goal is more difficult than if they had a shorter deadline. The research showed that this led people to allocate more resources, such as money and time, which can be a deterrent and is also not always necessary. Instead of setting long deadlines for yourself, think about creating shorter-term goals and deadlines to support yourself in successfully completing whatever end goal you have in mind.

Checkpoint

Are you doing yourself a disservice by setting long deadlines for yourself and your goals?

When it comes to dealing with procrastination there are a few other things that can help. If there are tedious jobs that you don't enjoy which you avoid and put off to the last minute, would it be possible to delegate those tasks or hire a virtual assistant to help you navigate them so you can focus on the things that you do enjoy? If this is not in the cards, is there a way to make those activities more enjoyable? When you still need to get those frustrating activities done, consider setting up a reward system for yourself. Something like, I am going to do the filing I have been putting off first thing at the start of the workday, and then I am going to walk to my favorite café to order my beverage of choice.

If you are procrastinating due to overwhelm or because you are afraid to get out of your comfort zone, incorporate activities to manage your stress and try breaking the work tasks into more bite-size pieces. Instead of saying something like, I am going to create the entire PowerPoint presentation today, how about, I am going to work on the outline for my PowerPoint presentation today, or I am going to get the first slide of my PowerPoint presentation done today? If you are looking to write a book but the concept is just too much, instead of thinking, wow, I need to write 50,000 words, shift that to, I am going to write 100 words a day. If that is still too much, how about, I am going to write 50 words 3 times a week? And get specific with when you are going to do it. Maybe it's 12:30, after lunch. When you link this new activity to a specific time and an activity that is already in place, it can be easier to stick with it. Once you get started, those 50–100 words can quickly turn into 500, 1000, 2000 or more words at a time and before you know it, you will have gotten to your goal. One thing that I like to ask myself is: *What can I do today that my future self will thank me for?*

Another method that may help with navigating procrastination is the Pomodoro Technique.[15] Francesco Cirillo came up with this technique, which involves the following:

1. Determine what your activity or task is.

2. Set a timer for 25 minutes.

3. Work for 25 minutes, aiming to avoid distraction.

4. Take a 5-minute break.

5. Take a longer break of 15–30 minutes after every four intervals completed.

The Pomodoro Technique may help you feel more motivated to get after a task if you know that you will need to work on it for only 25 minutes at a time. It may make larger projects more digestible, and it could be helpful if you are easily distracted or if you lose focus regularly.

Another key component for productivity is to decide what times and days are best for different tasks. Begin to notice which times of the day you have the most energy. During those high-energy times it might be best to focus on creative projects and meetings where you are interacting with others. At times of the day where you feel less energized, that could be a good time to do more cut-and-dry tasks and busywork like responding to emails. For me, my most creative ideas and productive work tend to happen in the morning. If I need to get a large chunk of writing done, if I am working on a keynote talk, or if I am looking to create content, the morning is the best time for me to do that. If I need to send out email invitations for podcast guests, or if I need to do some editing, afternoons work well for that. According to Slack's 2023 Workforce Index,[16] answers varied regarding the best times for peak productivity, but 71% of respondents reported that late afternoon was the worst time for productivity, with productivity dropping between 3 p.m. and 6 p.m. So, if you are looking to get those creative juices flowing, 4 p.m. on a Friday is probably not the best time.

> ### Checkpoint
>
> What time of the day do you feel most productive?

Quit multitasking

Have you ever played a game of "Simon Says" and had some-one give you instructions to do two or three things at once? For example, Simon says jump on one foot while rubbing your belly and tapping your nose. Now you may think that you can effectively do many different things at once, but how good of a job are you actually doing and how do you feel while you are doing them? Do you feel a bit overwhelmed or flustered? Have you ever found yourself trying to eat lunch while responding to an email while also talking to someone on the phone?

Recently, I was sending an email to an upcoming podcast guest while I was also telling my kids to get ready for soccer. My mind was in a bunch of places at once. The purpose of the email was to send a Zoom link for our meeting the following week. I hit the send button while scrambling out the door with my two kids so we wouldn't be late, feeling overwhelmed but happy I got that off my to-do list. Shortly after, I received an email from that upcoming guest saying that there was not a Zoom link in the email. I had forgotten to add the link, which was the entire purpose of the mes-sage. I jokingly responded, "That's what I get for multitask-ing," and sent the Zoom link out. This was not only slightly embarrassing, it also ended up requiring more time and effort than if I had just focused on one task at a time.

I know that multitasking is tempting, but research[17] has shown that it can negatively impact productivity. Switching between tasks requires effort and it takes more time to mentally shift. Whether or not you realize it, there is a switch cost. It can also increase errors and it can be dangerous in certain situations. Research[18] has shown that it can increase cortisol and the back and forth of our attention results in our brains burning through energy faster, so we end up with jumbled thinking and feeling wiped out.

I am sure you have experienced the urge to check your phone when you hear a ding or feel a vibration, no matter how important the task is that you are currently working on. There are so many pulls on our attention during the day that it is incredibly important for us to create healthy boundaries and implement strategies to minimize distractions. Turning off your cell phone notifications and scheduling times to check your email or social media accounts can help eliminate the mindless scrolling and dopamine-seeking behaviors that can be addictive and detrimental to your productivity and well-being. To support yourself with this you may need to keep your phone out of your workspace if you find yourself having a hard time focusing with it around. Really aim to create blocks of time where you focus on one task at a time, so you are not switching back and forth between activities.

When you are making your want-to-do list and your need-to-do list, make sure you are prioritizing the things that matter most. While talking on my Live Greatly podcast with Greg McKeown, bestselling author of *Effortless*[19] and *Essentialism*[20], he shared: "Figure out what's essential. You have to eliminate what's not essential and then, this word again, you have to make it as effortless as possible to do what matters most."

Aim to prioritize your high-return-on-investment (ROI) tasks and try having a clear schedule each day where you have specific times for all of the main activities that need to happen. If you are overwhelmed with mundane, time-consuming tasks with low ROI, see if there is room to delegate. The flexibility and autonomy that hybrid and remote work allow should give you the opportunity to schedule your day in alignment with what works for you. You may decide that in addition to scheduling time for video meetings, phone calls, and creative processes, you may want to put family time, an exercise session, or tidying up around the house into the calendar. This is where a work/life integration model comes in. You get to incorporate what works for you, your family, and your career. With effective organization, time management, and incorporating breaks into your everyday routine, you should see your productivity skyrocket.

Endnotes

1 Boubekri, M., Cheung, I.N., Reid, K.J., Wang, C.H. & Zee, P.C. (2014) Impact of Windows and Daylight Exposure on Overall Health and Sleep Quality of Office Workers: A Case-Control Pilot Study. *Journal of Clinical Sleep Medicine*, 10(06): 603–11. https://doi.org/10.5664/jcsm.3780
2 Jo, H., Song, C. & Miyazaki, Y. (2019) Physiological Benefits of Viewing Nature: A Systematic Review of Indoor Experiments. *International Journal of Environmental Research and Public Health*, 16(23): 4739. https://doi.org/10.3390/ijerph16234739

3 Ulrich, R.S. (1984) View Through a Window May Influence Recovery From Surgery. *Science*, 224(4647): 420–1. https://doi.org/10.1126/science.6143402

4 Lwin, M.O., Malik, S. & Neo, J.R.J. (2020) Effects of Scent and Scent Emission Methods: Implications on Workers' Alertness, Vigilance, and Memory under Fatigue Conditions. *Environment and Behavior*, 53(9): 987–1012. https://doi.org/10.1177/0013916520940804

5 Savavibool, N., Gatersleben, B. & Moorapun, C. (2018) The Effects of Colour in Work Environment: A Systematic Review. *Asian Journal of Behavioural Studies*, 3 (13): 149. doi:10.21834/ajbes.v3i13.152. https://www.researchgate.net/publication/327504773_The_Effects_of_Colour_in_Work_Environment_A_systematic_review

6 *Ibid.*

7 Slack (2023) *The surprising connection between after-hours work and decreased productivity.* https://slack.com/intl/en-gb/blog/news/the-surprising-connection-between-after-hours-work-and-decreased-productivity

8 DeskTime (2018) *The secret of the 10% most productive people? Breaking!* https://desktime.com/blog/17-52-ratio-most-productive-people

9 DeskTime (2021) *52/17 updated – people are now working and breaking longer than before.* https://desktime.com/blog/52-17-updated-people-are-now-working-and-breaking-longer-than-before

10 *Ibid.*

11 *Ibid.*

12 Sirois, F.M. (2023) Procrastination and Stress: A Conceptual Review of Why Context Matters. *International Journal of Environmental Research and Public Health,* 20(6): 5031. doi: 10.3390/ijerph20065031. PMID: 36981941; PMCID: PMC10049005. https://www.ncbi.nlm.nih.gov/pmc/articles/PMC10049005/#:~:text=Theory%20and%20evidence%20also%20suggest,avoidance%20%5B2%2C19%5D.

13 Loughborough University (2022) *Procrastination: the cognitive biases that enable it – and why it's sometimes useful.* https://www.lboro.ac.uk/news-events/news/2022/december/procrastination-why-its-sometimes-useful/

14 Zhu, M., Bagchi, R. & Hock, S.J. (2019) The Mere Deadline Effect: Why More Time Might Sabotage Goal Pursuit, *Journal of Consumer Research*, 45(5): 1068–84. https://doi.org/10.1093/jcr/ucy030

15 National Institute of Child Health and Human Development (2020) *The Pomodoro Technique: An Effective Time Management Tool.* https://science.nichd.nih.gov/confluence/pages/viewpage.action?pageId=160956640

16 Slack (2023) *The surprising connection between after-hours work and decreased productivity.* https://slack.com/intl/en-gb/blog/news/the-surprising-connection-between-after-hours-work-and-decreased-productivity

17 American Psychological Association (2006) *Multitasking: Switching costs.* https://www.apa.org/topics/research/multitasking

18 Levitin, D. J. (2015) *Why the modern world is bad for your brain.* *The Guardian.* https://www.theguardian.com/science/2015/jan/18/modern-world-bad-for-brain-daniel-j-levitin-organized-mind-information-overload

19 McKeown, G. (2021) *Effortless: Make It Easier to Do What Matters Most*, New York: Crown Currency.

20 McKeown, G. (2014) *Essentialism: The Disciplined Pursuit of Less*, New York: Crown Currency.

CHAPTER 8

Become a master choreographer for your remote or hybrid team

• • •

Think about the last music video or dance performance that you watched. Maybe it was the halftime show at the Superbowl or it could have been a musical or a video on YouTube. The dancers most likely looked in sync, like they had rehearsed their moves hundreds if not thousands of times, making their routine look natural and seamless. What you didn't see was all of the time and the effort they put in to get them to that point. You didn't see the growing pains, the missteps, and the challenges along the way. You didn't see the choreographer behind the scenes who had a vision of that end result even when they were just getting started. The choreographer who helped guide and instruct the dancers along the way, helping bring out the best in each one of them, resulting in a spectacular show that you ultimately got to enjoy. Getting to that place doesn't just happen overnight. In the beginning there are always setbacks and misinterpretations, but with communication, practice, and trust, the choreographer can create an environment for the group to dance gracefully together, anticipating the others' moves, knowing exactly what they need to do to be in harmony.

If you are currently a team leader or if you are an aspiring team leader, you are a master choreographer for each employee in your group and in your workplace. Every employee is going to have a different style, unique talents, and particular pain points. As a leader it is your responsibility to create a space where employees can maximize their potential. Where every member of your team is seen, included, and valued. Where each person is utilizing their gifts, contributing to the goals and mission of the team and organization. Now getting to that place is not always smooth or easy. There can be growing pains along the way, but as a leader your job is to help create a masterful dance in the end. Now there are some key things that a leader should incorporate to address common challenges while managing a remote or hybrid team, but first let's identify some of the common pain points you may be facing.

One issue leaders may face while overseeing a hybrid or remote team is trusting that their group members are maximizing their productivity without being able to actually see them working in an office setting. A 2022 study by Microsoft[1] showed that there can be a large disconnect between employees' actual productivity and their productivity perceived by their team leaders. Take a moment to think about your answer to the following question:

Do you think the hybrid or remote workers in your company or organization are more productive, less productive, or equally productive compared with the employees that regularly go into the office?

While some leaders may have concerns about hybrid or remote work diminishing productivity, in the Microsoft study the productivity signs via Microsoft 365 were increasing and 87% of employees surveyed reported that they were productive at work. (Those surveyed worked in a mix of environments, they were not just remote or hybrid remote workers.) That said, 85% of leaders surveyed said that changing to hybrid work resulted in them being challenged with having confidence in employees' productivity.

There are discrepancies in the results from research on productivity with remote work, with some results showing a negative impact and some showing a positive impact. According to a 2023 Goldman Sachs US Daily report,[2] the estimated results on the impact of remote work on productivity vary from –19% to +13%. These discrepancies could be influenced by many different aspects, including the type of work, how productivity was measured, the leadership and company culture, the happiness of the employees, the organization as a whole, and more. The tough part here is that at the end of the day, even if a remote worker is incredibly productive, the fact that they are not visibly seen in the company office doing the work unfortunately may lead to some distrust and concerns about their performance among team leaders. That said, transparency, optimal communication, and trust are necessities while managing remote teams.

Checkpoint

Do you trust the employees that you oversee as a leader? If not, how can you work to build more trust?

Optimal communication and great leadership go hand in hand, but how great a communicator are you? Even, if you think this is an area you excel in, it can be easy to unintentionally have the blinders on relating to how well you actually communicate. It can also be challenging to really gauge how others are responding to your style, especially when you are in a position of power. A 2021 study by SpiralMethod,[3] including 1,168 employees and 125 decision makers, showed a significant discrepancy between how leaders felt and how employees felt regarding communication. According to this study, 93% of the surveyed leaders believed they maintained a clear feedback loop with their team. That is a really high percentage, especially when 44% of the employees surveyed felt their company *did not* have a feedback loop established. If employees don't feel heard, problems can arise.

A 2022 report[4] shared by Microsoft showed that employees that didn't believe that feedback was driving change were more than twice as likely to consider leaving in the next year compared with those that did.

So, how can companies and team leaders overcome these obstacles and thrive in remote and hybrid work environments? Well, it starts with building awareness and fine-tuning your communication skills as a leader. While I was talking on my podcast with Robert Sutton, who is an organizational psychologist and professor of Management Science and Engineering in the Stanford Engineering School, we discussed friction in the workplace. One big factor Robert mentioned as a contributor to friction at work was oblivious leaders. Robert then went on to discuss how as power grows, unawareness of the impact you are having on others can grow as well. This can be a big problem in the workplace. If you have a leader that is regularly emailing and messaging their team at 8 o'clock on Friday night, or if they are continuously setting up long and unnecessary meetings, this can fuel stress, overwhelm, and unhappiness at work.

Checkpoint

Have you lost the larger perspective on how you are influencing others at work since taking on more responsibilities?

Get to know your dance partner

How well do you know the members of your team? Having excellent communication skills is incredibly important for all leaders, however it is even more critical for team leaders of remote or hybrid teams. Not having everyone under the same working roof means that issues can be more easily missed or get lost in translation. There have been times in my career where I received an email from a boss which I interpreted as being aggressive and disappointed, resulting in me stressing out and nervously preparing for a "big" conversation. However, when we connected face to face, the conversation was amicable and positive. Emotions and intentions can get lost when you are not able to see a person's face or hear the tone of their voice.

When I spoke on my podcast with Deb Cupp, the president of Microsoft Americas, we discussed some of the struggles with remote and hybrid work and she shared: "I think open communication is the most valuable thing that we can do between leaders and our people." Something important to recognize is that people communicate differently, they respond to communication differently, and they may interpret things differently than you would. Some things that you may take for granted may need to be expressed. The members of your team all have different learning styles, personal core values, unique upbringings, and individual experiences that will influence how they communicate and how they show up. As a team leader, it is your job to get to know your team and to understand what type of communication they respond to best.

Recognizing that not all people think like you can be a game changer for how you show up on your leadership journey.

So how can you set yourself up for effectively leading each member of your team based on their personality, skills, and values? With a remote or hybrid team, setting aside time for one-on-one conversations to discover what is important to them, what their personal mission is, and what their aspirations and goals are is imperative. It is also necessary to have informal check-ins during which you ask your team how you can help them and whether they need any support. Aim to schedule regular and reasonable checkpoints with your group without overscheduling unnecessary video meetings that can drain energy and become tedious. Once you really know each member of your group, you can be the master choreographer, giving them the space and trust to effectively execute their moves while meaningfully contributing to the success of the overall team. As a leader it is important that you guide the members of your group instead of trying to do all the moves for them. No one likes an overbearing dance partner or teacher who doesn't ever give them space.

Mentor, don't micromanage.

While I was talking on my podcast with John Foraker, the CEO of organic baby foods company Once Upon a Farm (one of its co-founders is actress Jennifer Garner), I asked him about what he thought some of the most important leadership skills and qualities for a healthy company culture and profitability were. He said: "To me, being a leader is about authenticity. It's about being yourself always. It's about being a great listener. Like really pausing and listening, and most importantly it's collecting and bringing together great people and just allowing them to unleash their greatness."

John and I then started talking about micromanaging and he went on to say: "And then for people who know they are micromanagers and are struggling with that, it is very counterproductive. If you have people who are working for you that need to be micromanaged constantly, that's the way that you get the best results, you may not have the right people, and you need to think about that. The right people definitely require guidance. They need to know where they are going. They want support. They want coaching. Everyone wants to feel like they are contributing on their own and not having every comma checked every time. It's hard to retain great people when you do that."

Checkpoint

Are you micromanaging? If so, what changes can you make to adopt a more beneficial leadership style?

Team building

Another potential challenge with remote work is effective team building. As a team leader you set the tone for a supportive and empowering work environment that prioritizes the well-being, happiness, and success of your team. So how can you do this? Consider establishing quarterly group meetings that are not work related, something like a virtual group coffee hour or lunch hour. Aim to create some wellness initiatives within your group to build community, possibly setting a new theme for each month. Your group can touch base with each other about their progress and you can share experiences together at your monthly meetings. You could incorporate incentives for employees that are engaged and successful. Incentives could be something like a gift card, paid time off, or something as simple as recognition.

Here is an example of what these monthly initiatives could look like:

January

Theme: Jump into the New Year

Description: Aim to get 10,000 steps a day. Depending on your budget and number of employees, you could consider getting employees pedometers to measure their steps.

February

Theme: Fresh Fruit and Vegetables

Description: Aim to get at least five servings a day of fruits and vegetables (at least two fruits and at least three vegetables). Employees should be encouraged to share recipes and track their progress.

March

Theme: Mindfulness

Description: This month is focused on mindfulness practices. Have your group try a one-month subscription to the same mindfulness and meditation app, with the goal of completing at least one activity on the app per day.

April

Theme: Get Outside

Description: This month is centered around getting outdoors and aiming to have at least 20 minutes of time outside per day. If you can spend that time in nature, even better.

May

Theme: Morning Routines

Description: Encourage at least 20 minutes of nourishing personal time before beginning work each day. This could be time for exercise, reading, meditation, or something else that will help you feel your best throughout the day.

June

Theme: Walking Meetings

Description: Encourage walking internal meetings in place of Zoom calls or standard computer-based meetings.

July

Theme: Fun

Description: Encourage and reward trying fresh activities like a new sport, a gardening club, or an outdoor exercise class.

August

Theme: Break Time

Description: Aim to have regular microbreaks incorporated into the workday. Put scheduled breaks onto the calendar.

September

Theme: Stand and Stretch

Description: Aim to get up to move and stretch every hour throughout the workday. Provide resources to online stretching and yoga classes.

October

Theme: Healthy Snacking

Description: Encourage healthy snacking options throughout the workday. Share snack ideas and consider having each member of the group share their favorite healthy snack.

November

Theme: Gratitude Practices

Description: Start a daily gratitude journal where you write down three things you are thankful for at the start of each day and then again at the end of each day. Employees can also have the option of sharing things they are thankful for within the group.

December

Theme: Connecting to Community

Description: Team members are encouraged to give back to a cause that is meaningful to them. Encourage volunteering and consider giving a day off to team members to volunteer someplace in their community.

While deciding which monthly initiatives would most benefit your group, make this a team effort by getting the team members involved in sharing ideas for themes. Depending on the size of your group, you can think about having each person come up with a weekly or monthly theme. Make it fun. As a leader, the members of your group are looking to you to set an example. Exemplify positive behaviors and practices for your team members by prioritizing your own well-being, setting healthy boundaries, and actively participating in wellness initiatives.

Be inclusive

Prioritizing diversity and inclusion within your organization and group is another critical component of optimal leadership where you are intentionally creating and embracing an environment with people from all different backgrounds, and with people that see the world differently than you. Building a diversified network outside of your group and team is also incredibly important. While talking with Dr. Michelle P. King on my podcast she shared: "Hey, the world of work has changed. Arguably one of the worst things you can do when it comes to building your informal network is to exclude people, because a diversified network is actually a great network, right, you're really going to build relationships with people who don't look like you. That's going to help you when it comes to your career."

Building awareness, emotional intelligence, and empathy

You can graduate at the top of your class with straight As and have an incredible amount of knowledge about an area, but if you lack social skills and the ability to interact with others, you will not be an optimal leader. During my training to become a physician assistant, I had to do clinical rotations with many different physicians and healthcare providers. Some were great, others resulted in me having experiences that were truly awful. Even if I was fascinated by the area of medicine that my rotation was in, if the supervising physician was condescending, rude, and intimidating to approach it would take away from my ability to learn, to do my best, and to get the most out of my experience. I even dreaded interacting with one of my rotation heads so much that I made up an excuse to get out of one of my shifts.

On the flip side, during my training if there was an area of medicine that didn't pique my interest but the physician overseeing me was engaging, encouraging, and supportive, it resulted in me thoroughly enjoying my rotation, regardless of the specialty. Interacting with a positive, supportive leader left me feeling excited to show up each day.

Once I graduated and I was officially practicing in healthcare, I interacted with many different types of healthcare providers with just as many different types of styles. I interacted with physicians who were incredibly smart but they were rude, and their bedside manner was nonexistent. While they had a lot of credentials after their name, these physicians would not thrive in a leadership role. I also knew physicians that were smart, and they also made patients feel at ease. They were approachable and supportive to their colleagues and the students they were mentoring. They would be more effective leaders, not because they were smarter but because they were smart *and* they were good with people.

Checkpoint

Think back to your favorite teachers and leaders. What do you notice about their people skills and how they made you feel?

Now even if you don't have some of these key people skills yet, the good news is that some of these skills can be developed. One skill that can have a significant impact on effective leadership is emotional intelligence. According to the *Merriam-Webster*[5] dictionary, emotional intelligence is defined as "the ability to recognize, understand, and deal skillfully with one's own emotions and the emotions of others (as by regulating one's emotions or by showing empathy and good judgment in social interactions)." The *Merriam-Webster*[6] dictionary defines empathy as "the action of understanding, being aware of, being sensitive to, and vicariously experiencing the feelings, thoughts, and experience of another." So how can you begin to increase emotional intelligence and empathy in your work/life?

The first step is by fostering awareness in the right way. As a leader, knowing yourself and understanding how you impact others is of the upmost importance. Some shocking research[7] showed that while 95%[8] of the people assessed thought they were self-aware, only 10–15% of those studied actually fit the criteria of being self-aware. The researchers looked at two key components of awareness: internal awareness and external awareness. Internal awareness encompasses how well we know and understand ourselves, while external awareness encompasses how well we understand how others view us. To grow in these areas, we need to work on self-improvement while also actively seeking feedback from others.

The research talked about how introspection, which is commonly suggested to build awareness, may actually hinder self-awareness and lead to ruminations and negativity, mainly because oftentimes it can be done incorrectly. The researchers suggested this is due to often asking "why" questions instead of more productive and helpful "what" questions. They found that people's well-being suffered when they frequently self-analyzed and they ended up being more depressed and anxious.

I think this may be due to people focusing on the wrong things while reflecting, all while creating unhelpful disempowering stories around *why* things didn't go the way they had hoped. Focusing your energy on this and believing those disempowering thoughts and stories can lead to uncomfortable feelings as well as potentially negatively impacting your mental health. Asking yourself things like "Why did I do that?" may lead to you getting stuck in the problem, instead of focusing on a solution and moving forward. If you focus on the *why* question, you may come up with many possible different reasons for why, many of which won't be factual, and some of which may just leave you feeling bad about yourself.

If you don't perform well in a meeting and you ask yourself "Why was I so bad out there?" you may go down a rabbit hole of negative self-talk, dwelling on things from the past, all while hypothesizing about the cause of your performance, which may not be true or helpful. If you allow your reflection and introspection to focus on things outside of your control, or if it leads you to believe unhelpful thoughts and restrictive views of yourself, it will not get you to where you want to be. A more future-based, solution-focused approach to building self-awareness can be more productive and empowering. This could look like reflecting on a situation by asking yourself, "What can I do differently next time?" Notice the difference in how you feel when you ask yourself these questions. The *what* question will most likely lead to a more optimistic, empowering feeling that supports positive action and growth.

To be a great leader, in addition to building internal awareness, you need to understand and seek out honest feedback from those around you. In the research[9] discussed above, the researchers suggested seeking feedback from loving critics, people who will be honest with you and who are looking out for your best interests. Getting feedback is not always comfortable, and more often than not it will be uncomfortable, especially in the beginning. Expect that and give yourself compassion and encouragement along the way by recognizing the huge return on investment for getting that feedback. While it may make you squirm a bit, getting true and honest feedback can help you take your career and leadership role to the next level. Aim to have regular checkpoints with yourself and with people you trust to keep you on track. It is also important to have a clear feedback loop so that employees can provide feedback about their leadership team without worrying that they will get into trouble or have it negatively impact their career.

Checkpoint

Is there a regular feedback loop in place so that your group or team can safely provide you with feedback?

Manage your emotions

In addition to working on building awareness, as a leader you need to learn how to deal with strong emotions. As human beings, it is natural to experience a wide variety of feelings in our lives; from emotions like sadness, anger, and worry to joy, gratitude, and relief. When you are faced with stressful moments at work, or while you are interacting with colleagues or clients, how do you handle it? How do your reactions and responses impact your team, your colleagues, and your clients?

Checkpoint

Do you allow your emotions to manage you, or do you manage your emotions?

Something that can be helpful to support you in navigating different emotions is when strong feelings surface, pause and recognize that strong emotions will pass. They are just passing through giving you feedback. They are visitors providing you with information. Allow your emotions to settle so that you can respond with a clear mind instead of reacting in a way you will later regret. Checking in with your future self is another tip that can help you gain a higher perspective.

In those challenging and stressful moments, ask yourself: "When I look back on this situation a week from now, what response will I be proud of?"

Building emotional intelligence can help you with decision making and it can help guide you to know how to respond appropriately in different situations. When you are interacting with others, remember that there are many ways to perceive a situation. Aim to try to see things from another person's point of view. Also, remember that you often don't know the full story. People can be going through hardships that you know nothing about. Every person on planet earth has their own unique challenges and setbacks that they are working through at different times in their lives. Recognize that you don't know everything. You could be wrong. You could be completely misinterpreting a situation. You could have a story running through your head that is 100% off base. This is why great communication is so important. If you have had a tough interaction with someone, or if you are in a tough situation, focus on growth, asking yourself: *What is the lesson for me here?*

Need another reason to make emotional intelligence a priority? Having emotional intelligence can help you be a better leader. Research[10] has shown that team members benefit from having leaders with emotional intelligence, and it even supports creativity and innovation. To enhance emotional intelligence and to build empathy, go into conversations with an open mind and utilize mindful active listening by bringing your attention and focus to the present moment. Focus on the person communicating with you instead of just preparing for what you should say next. Pay attention to what the person is saying and their nonverbal cues. You may notice that the person you are talking to seems upset, frustrated, or nervous and you can adjust your responses and approach as needed depending on the situation. Have compassion and be kind. Using these skills can help you navigate difficult conversations while also

building a company culture that is empowering, supportive, and successful.

Checkpoint

Notice what is happening with your internal dialogue and focus
the next time you are interacting with someone at work. Are
you present and engaged or are you mostly focused on what
you should say next?

Transparency

The tango is a cooperative dance which requires a leader
and a follower. It also includes improvisation. As a leader,
it is important to be transparent with your team about
expectations and job responsibilities, but you also need
to allow room for your team to improvise. People need to
have autonomy to be able to do their jobs in the way that
best suits their needs and talents. In order to trust that your
team is on top of their job responsibilities, so that you
don't need to check in on every little thing, you need to
get clear about what their responsibilities are and what
their coverage should be. Recognizing that there are
only a certain number of workable hours in the day, you
should be communicating what the top priorities are to
help employees properly manage their time. According to
research[11] by Microsoft, while 81% of employees believed
that getting support from their managers in prioritizing
their workload was important, only 31% reported getting

clear guidance from their managers during their one-on-one meetings.

While talking on my podcast with Martin G. Moore, co-founder of Your CEO Mentor, he shared: "I say that when people come into work each day, they want to know three things. For all the complexities and nuances of human interaction, we're pretty simple, right? What are your expectations of me? How am I performing against those expectations? What does my future hold?" The more clarity you can give your group around these areas, the better.

Something else to look at is this: how do you measure your team's productivity and success? Instead of measuring success by the amount of time clocked in, aim to have other measures of productivity which allow each employee to flex their unique talent muscles. During my conversation with Deb Cupp, president of Microsoft Americas, she said, "Not everybody is going to work in the same way and that's okay. Let's focus on the output." A key for managers leading remote teams is to stop worrying about *how* people are getting things done and instead focus on the results. Allow your workers to have the flexibility to get their work done in the way that is best for them.

Don't yell at your dance partner

As a leader, your communication style, your tone, and your word choices impact how well the information you are passing along is received. How you communicate will influence how people feel, which can also influence how they respond. If you think back to the worst boss you've ever had, the fact that they have claimed that spot probably has something to do with how they communicated and how they made you feel. While I was talking on my podcast with Claude Silver, chief heart officer for VaynerMedia, she shared: "Are we leaving people better than we found them? That's what I care about. Are we making someone's life easier in some way, shape, or form?"

As a leader, you are not always going to have good news to deliver. There are going to be tough conversations that need to be had and people are not always going to like what you tell them. That said, how you provide that information matters. When giving feedback, aim to have it be clear, concise, and specific. I used to be a proponent of the sandwich approach, where you start with something positive, then you share the area where there is room for improvement, and you finish with some encouraging words. While there is some research[12] supporting its potential benefits, this approach may also have a downside. It is also reported[13] that for some people, the sandwich approach may seem disingenuous, may create uncertainty about the messaging, or may be misinterpreted as all positive or all negative. In that case, it is suggested to provide positive feedback in a genuine stand-alone manner to build rapport and then to provide negative feedback separately in a clear and actionable way.

I believe a portion of how feedback is received depends on the relationship and trust between the people having the conversation as well as the delivery and the personality of the person receiving the feedback. There are times when I appreciate hearing the positive mixed in with the areas where there is room for improvement, and then there are other times when I just want to get the negative or constructive feedback out of the way. In all of these situations, being specific and clear helps. If your boss said, "These slides just won't work. Get new ones to me by tomorrow," you would probably be left feeling confused, frustrated, and unsure about which area you need to adjust. A better approach would be saying something like, "Ideally, we need the messaging in these slides to be short and concise, so would you be able to turn those longer text slides into shorter bullet points and get it to me by tomorrow in time for the meeting? I really appreciate your help with this." The first feedback example was vague and unproductive. The second example was constructive, clear, and solution-focused while also making the person on the receiving end feel valued.

When employees feel valued, they are more likely to feel fulfilled in their jobs, resulting in higher employee retention, happier employees, a better product, and happier customers.

Checkpoint

How can you improve how you provide feedback to your group? Are you providing positive feedback as well as feedback on areas where there is room for growth?

Endnotes

1 Microsoft (2022) *Hybrid Work Is Just Work. Are We Doing It Wrong?* https://www.microsoft.com/en-us/worklab/work-trend-index/hybrid-work-is-just-work?wt.mc_id=AID_M365Worklab_Corp_HQ_Charter

2   Goldman Sachs (2023) *Remote Work, Three Years Later.* https://www.gspublishing.com/content/research/en/reports/ 2023/08/28/6fd0a8a0-3831-4ace-b577-a93337f01ec8.html

3   SpiralMethod (2021) Remote work works – new study indicates 80% of leaders and employees saw increased productivity but highlights disconnect with communication and transparency. https:// www.prnewswire.com/news-releases/remote-work-works---new-study-indicates-80-of-leaders-and-employees-saw-increased-productivity-but-highlights-disconnect-with-communication-and-transparency-301341901.html

4   Microsoft (2022) *Hybrid Work Is Just Work. Are We Doing It Wrong?* https://www.microsoft.com/en-us/worklab/work-trend-index/ hybrid-work-is-just-work?wt.mc_id=AID_M365Worklab_ Corp_HQ_Charter

5   Merriam-Webster (2024) *Emotional intelligence.* https://www. merriam-webster.com/dictionary/emotional%20intelligence

6   Merriam-Webster (2024) *Empathy.* https://www.merriam-webster. com/dictionary/empathy

7   Eurich, T. (2018, January 4) *What Self-Awareness Really Is (and How to Cultivate It).* https://hbr.org/2018/01/what-self-awareness-really-is-and-how-to-cultivate-it

8   Eurich, T. (2017, December 9) *Increase your self-awareness with one simple fix.* https://www.youtube.com/watch?v=tGdsOXZpyWE

9   Eurich, T. (2018, January 4) *What Self-Awareness Really Is (and How to Cultivate It).* https://hbr.org/2018/01/what-self-awareness-really-is-and-how-to-cultivate-it

10 Ivčević, Z., Moeller, J., Menges, J.I. & Brackett, M.A. (2020) Supervisor Emotionally Intelligent Behavior and Employee Creativity. *The Journal of Creative Behavior*, 55(1): 79–91. https:// doi.org/10.1002/jocb.436

11 Microsoft (2022) *Hybrid Work Is Just Work. Are We Doing It Wrong?* https://www.microsoft.com/en-us/worklab/work-trend-index/ hybrid-work-is-just-work?wt.mc_id=AID_M365Worklab_ Corp_HQ_Charter

12 Procházka, J., Ovcari, M. & Ďuriník, M. (2020) Sandwich feedback: The empirical evidence of its effectiveness. *Learning and Motivation*, 71: 101649. https://doi.org/10.1016/j.lmot.2020.101649
13 Emory, Cynthia L. MD, MBA (January 2019) Pearls: Giving and Receiving Feedback. *Clinical Orthopaedics and Related Research*, 477(1): 35–6. https://doi.org/10.1097/corr.0000000000000538

PART III

Connection, community, and boundaries

CHAPTER 9

Spending quality time with all of your dance partners

● ● ●

I have yet to meet a parent who has not experienced parental guilt in one form or another. While it is really common, it can also be super tough to deal with. So where does this guilt come from? Some of it can be feedback for us on areas that require more of our attention or insights into where we are spending our time. But I believe that a lot of this guilt can also stem from expecting too much of ourselves, or trying to live up to impossible expectations or a vision of what we think a "perfect" parent looks like. Even though it may appear like people on social media or characters on TV have it all figured out, there is not a one-size-fits-all approach to being a great parent while also having a flourishing career. That said, to discover what works for you and your family, you need to have regular checkpoints with yourself and with your loved ones. You also need to be able to share concerns and needs with your boss when appropriate. As a remote or hybrid worker, open communication is critical. Even when it is uncomfortable, you need to be able to ask for what you need and for what is best for you and your family dynamic.

When it comes down to it there are going to be times in your life where you feel stretched too thin. When you wish you could be in more places than one. Even when you try to do everything right, it sometimes won't feel like enough. Navigating spending enough high-quality time with family and friends while working and having personal time as well is more of an art form than an exact science. That said, one thing is for sure: to thrive in your family life, you need to make it a priority. There is not a perfect way to do this, but it does require consistently evaluating where things are at and making adjustments and shifts when needed. And sometimes just when you think you have got it down and things are going smoothly, something changes.

When you are working on integrating family and kids into your everyday work/life, trial and error is inevitable and necessary, so you need a lot of self-compassion while finding what works best for you and for your loved ones. It is important to be kind to yourself throughout this process and recognize that this can be a tricky area for many. I remember after I gave a keynote, I walked off stage and was gathering my things when I was approached by an audience member. I had been talking about thriving in work and life and part of that was discussing boundaries and integrating family into your everyday. He asked me how he could know what the right amount of time was to spend with his child. He said that the amount of time he spent with his son never seemed to be enough and his son always wanted to spend more and more time with him than he could offer. I think he was probably hoping that I would give him an exact number and say something like, "You should spend three hours with your son per day." What I actually said was that there is not an exact amount of time that would automatically make everyone happy or that would meet each person's needs. I went on to say that this was something that they would need to figure out themselves based on the unique needs of his child and his work/life situation as well.

Another important piece of the puzzle is trying to make sure that the time you have with your children is *high quality*, meaning that you are fully present and not distracted with other matters by consistently checking your phone or shooting off emails on your laptop. If you are continuously glancing at your phone, or if it is out on the table when you are playing a board game with your family, you are dividing your attention and you could be giving off the message, "I'm bored, this isn't that important, I have other things I need to be focusing on right now." Implement boundaries with your phone and your attention, especially when you are in family mode.

Integrating family and friends into your remote workday and life is an ever-evolving process that will change with time. While there isn't a magic amount of time spent with your loved ones that will solve all of your problems, there are some things that can help. Have regular checkpoints with your family to see how everyone is feeling and schedule quality time to be together and reconnect. Ask your family or kids some things that they would love to do and carve out time to enjoy those things together. Add in some fun family rituals like making dinner together on Friday nights or enjoying a special breakfast together on Sunday mornings. Incorporate mindfulness to help your attention be in the present moment. Appropriately manage your time, set boundaries, delegate appropriately, and prioritize family by having important family events added into your schedule. When you do what you need to do so that the time you have with your loved ones is high quality, you will feel more ful-filled in your family life while working from home.

Checkpoint

What are some activities your family or children would love to do with you that you can arrange and add to your schedule this week?

While I was recording a podcast episode with Dr. Susan Ratay, a friend and classmate from my integrative medicine fellow-ship, she provided a great analogy about navigating work and family. Imagine juggling life-like juggling balls. Some of the balls are made of glass and some are made of rubber. It's okay to let the rubber ones drop knowing that they will still be there when you are ready to get to them, but make sure you don't drop the breakable glass ones. When you are looking at everything you would like to do in a day, notice which areas are the glass balls and which are the rubber ones that can be set aside for the moment. Perhaps the bathrooms won't get cleaned that week or the laundry will wait a bit so you can have the time you need with your family and loved ones, and that is more than okay. If there is a lot of stuff to do around the house, make it a family affair. We have a lot of family folding sessions on the weekends where we are able to watch a fun show together while sorting and folding laundry.

At times you need to get creative with managing your time to maximize spending time with loved ones. There have been days when my to-do list was incredibly long and my kids asked me to play something with them. While I wanted to say yes, it felt like I was carrying a heavy weight of things that needed to happen before I could relax and give myself the freedom to play with my kids. A key for me was recognizing which of those things really needed to get done and which things were more on my *want*-to-do list versus *need*-to-do list. I noticed that I sometimes put a lot of pressure on myself to get an unrealistic number of things done in one day than was practical. To be able to freely enjoy saying yes when my kids asked me to play something, I needed to tweak my expectations to make space for play time and down time. If there were high-priority tasks that couldn't wait, I would say that I would love to play after I took care of those necessities and I would give a time frame to set expectations. If I realized that the things on my list could wait, I could say yes to enjoy spending time with my kids right then without having to carry the weight of self-imposed pressure. I also realized that my to-do list didn't only need to include tedious tasks or errands that needed to happen. I needed to add play time with my kids onto the list!

> ### Checkpoint
>
> Are you making family time a key part of your to-do list?

You aren't meant to do it alone

A key component to thriving in your family life with hybrid or remote work is knowing when to ask for help. There are only 24 hours in a day and most people are awake for 16 of them. This leaves you with 960 active minutes each day to incorporate all the things that are meaningful to you. There is an incredible amount of potential for amazing high-quality moments and experiences in those 960 minutes, but you can't do everything all at once. So, how can you maximize how you are spending your time? You have to know your limits, establish effective time management, and delegate in order to feel fulfilled in your family life.

Back when I made the transition from being a stay-at-home mom to being in the workforce again, I struggled with asking for help with stuff around the house. I was used to handling all the grocery shopping, the cooking, the dishes, the laundry, and the tidying up because I had been home and I had the time to do it. When I started a new job, I found that I still expected myself to be able to handle the same responsibilities at home. What I quickly realized was that effectively doing all that I had been doing while being a stay-at-home mom, while also starting a new job and wanting to spend quality time with my husband and kids, was just not practical. Trying to do all of that was making me feel overwhelmed. I needed to loosen the reins on some of the household tasks that I had claimed when I was home more, and I needed to ask for help. It wasn't that any of those things around the house were being asked of me or expected of me, my husband was more than happy to help, but I was the one putting the pressure on myself to get all those things done.

You are not meant to do it all alone. Asking for help is key to being able to thrive in your relationships and family life.

> ### Checkpoint
>
> What area in your home life would benefit from you asking for help?

Can family and work actually complement each other?

Do you view work and family as totally separate? Rather than viewing work on one side and family on the other, the flexibility of remote and hybrid work offers an incredible opportunity to integrate family time into your day. A valuable method to add more family-related moments into your day is to use your calendar to schedule important times with loved ones. If you have children that are home while you are working, you could use some of your breaks to spend time with them. Read them a book or go outside for 10 minutes to play an activity outdoors. Think about using a sign on your door for alerting your kids and family to when they can come in and when your office is a *DO NOT ENTER* zone. Including your kids in your remote work when appropriate and teaching them about what you are doing can be a win-win for everyone.

In addition to scheduling time with your children if you have them, schedule time with friends and family to grab lunch, go for a walk, get coffee, or do other enjoyable activities mid-day. My husband Brian and I have found that our evening date nights have lessened as our kids have gotten older, with more sporting events and family activities in the evenings and weekends, so we decided that we were going to increase our lunch dates. We both work remotely, so lunchtime has been a great opportunity for us to spend some solo time together.

Checkpoint

What is something you can do to integrate more family into your remote workday?

Protect your family time

Time with your loved ones is sacred. It is something that you need to value, protect, and preserve. Work can get busy. Life can get busy. But don't let the hustle and bustle of the everyday make you lose sight of what is most important to you. Again, this is where having regular checkpoints with yourself can be helpful. If you have been struggling with making quality time for your family, you can change that. Start putting in place better boundaries. Have a set time that you close up the laptop for the day. After you log out of work, incorporate rituals that bring your family together, like making dinner together or dancing to some music while cleaning up.

Research[1] has shown that eating frequent family meals together supports children's and adolescents' mental health and it has been associated with less depression, less alcohol and substance use, less disordered eating, and less violent behavior. This research has also shown that frequent family meals may increase self-esteem, grade point average, and commitment to learning. The environment where you gather matters too. Research[2] has shown that a better atmosphere and more conversation during mealtimes have been related to decreased depressive symptoms in children.

Encourage active conversations while you are with your family. Have family members silence their phones and institute a "no phones at the table" rule. The benefits of regularly gathering with your family for meals are huge. Make high-quality family mealtimes a top priority.

Checkpoint

How many family meals are you having per week? How can you increase this number?

Other ways to deepen connection with family is to get a change of scenery with your loved ones and to set out on some new fun, shared adventures. Research[3] shows that travel may help strengthen family bonds, boost communication, reduce divorce, and increase well-being. So, make sure you are actually using your vacation time and personal time off. Other things you can do to promote an optimal family life include letting the people in your life know that you care about them and love them. Leave notes for your family and think of small ways that you can show them how much they mean to you. Discover shared interests with your kids or loved ones and come up with ways that you can enjoy these things together. Consider instituting a regular family game night. Think about learning something new together to have more joined experiences that promote bonding. Maybe you and your family want to take a cooking class together? Maybe you want to learn pickleball, golf, or start a garden? If there are certain things that your kids or family enjoy which are not really your thing, have them tell you about it and show them support by participating in some of these activities, even when they are not your favorite. By making these things a priority, you are showing those in your life that you value and appreciate them.

Take some time to reflect on where things are currently at in your family life, and how things are going in the following areas. If things are not where you would like them to be, focus on the solution. What can you do differently?

- Are you incorporating mindfulness into your family life?
- Are you setting intentions before you step into your family time to help you be fully engaged?
- Are you utilizing active listening with your family?
- Are you giving your family the attention and focus they deserve?
- Are you on your phone or computer a lot during family time?
- Are you making time for the things that really matter to you and your family?
- Are you using your vacation time and personal time off to enjoy family time?
- Do you have family rituals that help you connect?

Endnotes

1 Harrison, M.E., Norris, M.L., Obeid, N., Fu, M., Weinstangel, H., & Sampson, M. (2015). Systematic review of the effects of family meal frequency on psychosocial outcomes in youth. *Canadian family physician Medecin de famille canadien, 61*(2), e96–e106. https://www.ncbi.nlm.nih.gov/pmc/articles/PMC4325878/

2 Kim, Y.S., Lee, M.J., Suh, Y.S. & Kim, D.H. (2013) Relationship Between Family Meals and Depressive Symptoms in Children. *Korean Journal of Family Medicine, 34*(3): 206–12. doi: 10.4082/kjfm.2013.34.3.206. PMID: 23730488; PMCID: PMC3667228. https://ncbi.nlm.nih.gov/pmc/articles/PMC3667228/

3 Durko, A. & Petrick, J.F. (2013) Family and Relationship Benefits of Travel Experiences: A Literature Review. *Journal of Travel Research, 52*(6): 720–30. https://doi.org/10.1177/0047287513496478

CHAPTER 10

Choosing the best dance partners

● ● ●

I am not much of a dancer. I mean, I'm not terrible, I can hold my own while dancing with my kids and husband in our kitchen and I can do the Macarena at a wedding, but dancing in general was never my strong suit. I remember back when I was about 10 years old and my parents had signed me up for a jazz class. I dreaded having to go and I would try to make up excuses to get out of it. My stomach hurt. I had too much homework. Whatever I tried, my mom would see right through my ulterior motive and before I knew it, I would be shaking my hands and moving my feet with a move they called the "shimmies" while a line of girls and the teacher watched. I always naturally gravitated more towards sports, so I was 100% out of my element in that class.

That said, one night many years later I found myself in a very awkward situation where I was dancing around a classroom to interpretive music with a group of people. There were some people doing moves that looked like they were rolling around on the floor. Others were doing yoga poses. And some had dance moves that even looked choreographed. As I moved my way around the room, trying my best to "dance" through the uncomfortable feelings that were surfacing, some of the other dancers would get into my personal space. Some even tried to make long, extended eye contact with me before flowing away. No, this was not a dream, and it was not a dare, I actually volunteered for this exercise. During an in-person training week for my integrative medicine fellowship, we were presented with the opportunity to participate in this optional one-hour interpretive dance program. I would normally have declined the offer, but some friends in my class were going and they asked me to join them, so I decided to face my fear and try it out.

When we arrived, we were told that the goal of the session was to move around the room, dancing with people you didn't know, getting in their space, and then dancing away when you wanted to. If someone danced into your space and you didn't like it or you just wanted to move on, you were told to say "No thank you" or just "No" and then dance or move away. Now, this was definitely not what I was expecting, and when I heard about the assignment, I thought, what have I gotten myself into? Even though the thought of leaving crossed my mind, it seemed too late for that, having already made the commitment to my friends, so hesitantly I went with it. Was it uncomfortable? Yes. Did it make me take myself much less seriously? Also, yes.

This creative exercise was meant to remind us that we can establish and implement boundaries. You can say no. You can walk away. You can take your dance moves over to someone that is more your style. You can choose to dance alone. You have control around who you choose to spend your free time with. You are in control of your space.

So, how do the people that you are "dancing" with in your work and your life make you feel? Do they bring out the best in you or do they contribute to keeping you stuck with unhelpful habits, patterns, and beliefs? Do they support you in making healthy lifestyle choices? The people you choose to spend your time with are influencing you. They are impacting you whether you are fully aware of it or not. I talked earlier about how emotions are contagious, well happiness is contagious too! A groundbreaking study[1] showed that if a friend who lives within a mile of you becomes happy, you have a 25% higher likelihood of being happy too. The people you surround yourself with can empower you or they can hold you back and keep you stuck. Your social connections are impacting your choices and your behaviors for better or for worse.

In addition to our moods, studies have shown the impact that relationships have on our health in other ways. Research[2] has shown that obesity may spread via social connections, with a person's likelihood of being obese going up by 57% if a friend became obese and by 37% if a spouse became obese. Research has shown that friends' lifestyle choices also have an impact, and this starts early on in life. An example of this can be seen with the impact of having friends that smoke cigarettes at an early age. We have all heard about the risks of peer pressure and research[3] has shown that adolescents with friends that smoke are more likely to pick up smoking than those that have friends that do not smoke.

I remember as a kid my parents would do their best to guide me towards spending time with friends with healthy interests. Now, as a parent myself, I understand why. As an adult, you probably don't have someone guiding your choices around who you spend your time with anymore, so you are in the driver's seat here. Spending your free time making friends at the local pub or at the bar down the street will most likely not be the best choice for supporting you in having a healthy lifestyle. However, if you make some friends in a new fitness class, in a healthy cooking class, or while volunteering for a cause you believe in, you are setting yourself up for a friend group that will be more likely to promote a healthy lifestyle or participate in things that are meaningful to you.

To create and deepen friendships and beneficial relationships in a work setting, you can investigate different networking groups that are in alignment with your career to expand your horizons and gain support from people dealing with similar issues. When you surround yourself with people that support you, uplift you, and embrace interests or a lifestyle in alignment with your values, you are supporting optimal well-being and success in all areas of your life.

Checkpoint

Are your current relationships bringing out the best in you?

Boundaries with your friends

You may be thinking, well how do I know who to be spending time with? So much of having healthy and empowering relationships comes down to feelings and whether those in your life are supporting you and valuing you. To gain perspective on this, it can be helpful to begin to notice how you feel after spending time with those in your work/life. Do you regularly finish up hanging around a person or a group of people and feel depleted or grouchy? Do you find yourself complaining more or talking negatively about others around certain people? Do you tend to worry more around certain people? If you notice that behaviors that you don't like come creeping out when you are with a certain person or in a particular group, it's time to reevaluate who you are spending your time with. Some people may have been great during a part of your life, but if they aren't in alignment with who you want to be, and more importantly, if you regularly don't feel good after spending time with them, it's time to rethink where you are allocating your time.

Relationships are like driving a manual car. There will be times when you need to shift gears to get to where you want to go. Do you feel excited when a friend or relative reaches out to get together? Do they encourage you and celebrate your wins? Do you feel happy or relaxed after spending time with them? Do they support you and value you? Are they reliable? Do you trust them? The people that you answer "yes" to when you ask yourself those questions are people that are likely going to result in high-quality relationships. All relationships require focus, time, and energy, so if you are looking to build or strengthen relationships, effort and intention are required.

Checkpoint

What relationships would you like to allocate more time for? What can you do today to support those relationships?

Of course, work, life, and people aren't perfect, and there are bound to be people in your life that you need to interact with that you would rather not. Maybe it's a relative that always makes you feel inferior or perhaps it's a boss or colleague that makes you want to quit your job and move to Hawaii.

Regardless, go into those interactions using the stress-management and mindset tools you now have in your toolbox. Focus on the things that are inside of your control, which is you. Remember, you can't control other people's choices. Use mindfulness and deep breathing to make sure that you don't get sucked into other people's drama or unhelpful patterns and stay true to who you are. If you ever need to stand up for yourself, call on your inner Yoda and do it from a place of calm.

Remember: respond, don't react. Don't let someone else's behavior or choices result in you showing up as a less than optimal version of yourself. Draw on empathy and compassion. While you can't completely control how people treat you, you can influence them based on how you show up. Do you remember the Loving-Kindness Meditation you learned earlier on? If you are holding onto resentment or anger towards others, try it. Forgiveness frees your mind and body from holding onto emotions that are only hurting you.

Checkpoint

Who is someone you could benefit from forgiving?

When you say no (and it can be in a polite, respectful way), you are protecting the things that are meaningful to you. If you always respond to emails at 9 p.m. and on Sundays, guess what? People will expect you to respond in the late evening and on the weekends. By setting clear boundaries and letting your colleagues know that you don't check emails on the weekends or after a certain hour each evening, you make space for the other things that are high on your core values list. This is also applicable to your personal life. If you are overcommitting and saying yes to everyone, you are heading towards overwhelm, stress, and disharmony.

When things picked up with my business, I needed to prioritize the aspects that I was committing to in my personal life, to make sure I was reserving time for the things that were most important and meaningful to me. When I was asked if I was interested in taking on a volunteer opportunity, I knew that it wasn't the best time and that I would feel stretched too thin, and I politely declined. Saying no to this gave me the opportunity to say yes to other things that I was really excited about, like volunteering at my kids' schools and playing tennis with friends each week.

Saying no when necessary is not rude, it is wise. You deserve respect and you deserve to be happy. It's time to claim it. By prioritizing yourself and prioritizing your time, you will end up living a much more fulfilling and meaningful life.

Checkpoint

Where are you saying "yes" in your personal life when you should really be saying "no"?

Endnotes

1 Fowler, J.H. & Christakis, N.A. (2008) Dynamic spread of happiness in a large social network: longitudinal analysis over 20 years in the Framingham Heart Study, *British Medical Journal*, 337: a2338 https://www.bmj.com/content/337/bmj.a2338

2   Christakis, N.A. & Fowler, J.H. (2007) The Spread of Obesity in a Large Social Network over 32 Years. *The New England Journal of Medicine*, 357(4): 370–9. https://doi.org/10.1056/nejmsa066082

3   Simons-Morton, B.G. & Farhat, T. (2010) Recent Findings on Peer Group Influences on Adolescent Smoking. *The Journal of Primary Prevention*, 31(4): 191–208. https://doi.org/10.1007/s10935-010-0220-x

CHAPTER 11

Developing your dance troupe

· · ·

Have you ever been in a situation where you're working remotely, it's 5 p.m., and you've just realized that you're still in your pajama pants and you haven't left your house that day? While this may not be a big issue if it happens once in a while, if it is your typical workday, it is setting you up for feelings of isolation and loneliness. As human beings we have an innate need for real social connection and community. We thrive when we regularly see people, have in-person interactions and conversations.

Now don't freak out, but a study[1] even showed that lack of connection could be more harmful than smoking, obesity, and high blood pressure. Solid relationships and a sense of community are good for us in so many ways. Having social connections improves the quality of your life and may even lengthen it.[2] You probably know well that working remotely has the potential to be isolating, but by intentionally building connection, implementing healthy habits and patterns, and forming a sense of community, you will position yourself to thrive in all aspects of your work/life.

Building community in your personal life

I was recently participating in a new fitness class while on vacation with a small group of about five women and when

I arrived, I could tell that the other women all knew one another. As I got my mat set up, the instructor, let's call him George, went out of his way to make me feel comfortable and at ease by introducing himself right as I came in. He seemed relaxed and happy, which helped me get to a place where I was feeling relaxed too. Later, while we were holding our planks, George was telling us how excited he was about his daughter coming in that weekend to visit him. He said that she really enjoyed coming out because she worked remotely, so it could get lonely for her. He went on to say that she lived out of state alone with her cat, and while she really liked her job, it could be isolating at times. He mentioned how he had been encouraging her to break up her day with activities outside of the house where she would interact with people and ultimately form a community. Being in the fitness industry, he had naturally suggested that she join a midday fitness class. George then went on to say how so many people in his classes had ended up forming friendships and community when they initially came in hesitantly, not knowing anyone. He then referred to the women in the class as an example of this. He mentioned that the hardest part for most people was coming to the first class without knowing anyone.

Trying a new activity or a new group can always be a bit nerve racking, but once people make it to the first class, the next one is easier. They start seeing some familiar faces, and if they commit and come in week after week, those people end up becoming a part of their community. Some may even become close friends, and once those connections are built, people start to really look forward to those classes. Creating community in your personal and professional life takes effort and consistency, but the rewards are well worth it.

Checkpoint

How can you add in more social interactions during your remote workday?

If you are looking to form a deeper sense of community and connection in your life, optimal communication is key. What is the quality of your communication with your friends, family, and others in your life?

While chatting on my podcast with Alexandra Carter, negotiation expert, clinical professor of law and director of the Mediation Clinic at Columbia Law School, she talked about why we should try to avoid asking questions that start with the word "Why." If you ask someone why they did something, they can get defensive. Alex shared that she instead starts her questions with her "two magic words: Tell me." She used this method to communicate with her husband during the COVID-19 pandemic about who got the office with the door. Her husband had the office, but Alex wanted it because she spent more time on work calls than her husband. At first, she asked her husband in a moment of frustration: "*Why* do you have the office with the door?" which was not successful. Then, after regrouping a few days later, she said to her husband: "Let's sit down and I'd love for you to *tell me* your schedule for the week." After looking at their schedules and noting that Alex had a lot of interviews and podcasts arranged where her husband had more solo work, he said, "You know what? It looks like this week you should be in the office with the door." Alex eventually permanently relocated to the office with the door and her husband created an office in their attic, which worked well for their family dynamic.

Another way to make sure the people in your life feel seen and heard is to use the power of gratitude. Make sure to say "thank you" and use words of encouragement to those who support you.

Building community at work

What is the quality of your communication with your colleagues as a hybrid or remote worker? For some people, not being in a group office setting can lead to fears of being left out, especially if other colleagues are working in an office building together. As a remote worker, building rapport and trust without being face to face with your team requires effort and intention. Creating and embracing a culture where all team members are valued and treated with respect is also critical. As a remote or hybrid worker, do you feel like you are being treated well by your coworkers?

Unfortunately, a study[3] showed that remote workers were more likely to feel mistreated by their colleagues. This is just one reason why optimal communication is key. Never assume that others know what you are thinking or what you are working on. Assumptions just open the door for miscommunication and tension. When you have effectively built a personal connection with a team member or colleague, they will feel safer asking for help and sharing their concerns. Talking about personal things and pain points requires trust.

If you are looking to build connection, aim to get to know some of your colleagues on a personal level in a more informal setting. People respond to different communication mechanisms in different ways, so it could be helpful to add in an informal one-on-one phone call to get to know each other, which may take the pressure off and will feel different from traditional video meetings. People may let their guard down a bit more with phone calls versus video calls, and they can relax because they don't have to worry about their appearance or their location while having a conversation. There is also less stimulation with phone calls, so they just need to focus on your voice.

Research[4] has shown that voice-only communication increased the ability to accurately utilize empathy and it helped people more accurately identify the emotions of the person they were talking to. This means that you may be able to more accurately interpret how someone is feeling through just hearing their voice compared with a situation where you solely see someone or where you are able to utilize all your senses in an interaction. On top of this, phone calls can be really convenient. You could be taking a relaxing walk while chatting on the phone, or still be in your pajamas for an early morning call without having to think twice about it. In addition to phone calls, utilizing messaging apps or other communication platforms for informal communication with colleagues can help you stay connected during the workday. Setting regular meetings and check-ins, having more informal catchups, and even sending daily agendas and wrap-up emails can be helpful to make sure everyone feels up to date and included.

While video meetings do have a time and a place, they should be used with the awareness that when they are too frequent, too long, and when they consistently have a lot of people on the call, it can fuel Zoom fatigue and stress.

Research[5] has shown that people felt more connected when video meetings were short, frequent, and with fewer people compared with meetings that were long and filled with lots of people. The researchers also found that when meetings got longer and more frequent, people felt more fatigued and less connected. Too many video conferences also may reduce life satisfaction and fuel stress while negatively impacting mental health. This research also showed that people felt as though their social skills were not as good in video conferencing compared with in-person interactions.

These are all important aspects to consider when you are looking to build relationships in a virtual setting. There are unique benefits that we get with in-person interactions that cannot be replicated with video conferencing, so when possible, try to make time for an in-person meeting, conference, or get-together, even if it is just once a year, to deepen those connections even more.

Checkpoint

How do you tend to respond to virtual meetings? Do they tend to drain you more than other types of communication? What adjustments can you make to address this?

I have had a lot of practice with effectively building connection in a virtual environment through my Live Greatly podcast as well as with pre-booking calls for my speaking business with event planners, speaking agents, CEOs, and more. With my podcast, I have a short amount of time to build rapport with my guests, so that they feel comfortable diving into all different kinds of personal topics. I find that the more relaxed and at ease I am coming into these conversations, the more my authentic self comes through. When I am not focused on saying the right thing or doing the right thing, the conversation flows and evolves more naturally, and it is easier to get to know the person on the other end and form a connection.

When I started my podcast, I had my questions scripted out, and I felt a sense of pressure when I first met my guests. With a lot of practice under my belt, I realized that I didn't need to script things out. I liked the ability to go with the flow and let the conversation happen naturally while pulling from some general topics that I knew I wanted to touch on. To get to a place where great conversations happen, it has been important to establish some sort of a bond with a guest before I hit "record". To help with this, I never jump right into the business component when we start talking. I like to start informally by casually chatting about things like where we are from, and other snippets about where things are at in our lives. I approach this part with honesty and genuine interest, without planning it out or overthinking it, and I try to just let myself show up authentically as I am. I am always surprised by how often the allotted 5–10 minutes I give for this turns into 15 or 20 minutes of chatting before I hit the record button because mutual interests and connections are found and there are more and more things we are excited to talk about.

If you get nervous when meeting someone virtually for the first time, or before important meetings, you are not alone. When I have felt nerves pop up before having a highly visible guest on my show or before an important meeting, I remind myself that all I need to do is show up as me. Don't try to be someone you are not. You just need to be you, you don't need to be or appear perfect, and things will go as they should. You can also support yourself in getting that feeling of ease and calm by doing some intentional activities before these important virtual meetings, like going for a walk outside or getting in a workout to clear your head and get some endorphins flowing. And like all things, it does get better with practice.

> ### Checkpoint
>
> How can you set yourself up for feeling relaxed and at ease during virtual meetings?

In the world of remote work, pay attention to how you feel after different types of virtual meetings and get-togethers. Do you enjoy some and not others? Do you feel drained with certain types of virtual engagements? Research[6] has shown that Zoom fatigue may be more prevalent for women compared with men and it can be due to being overloaded with nonverbal communication cues. This research also shows that having video conferences for work-related matters is more fatiguing than having video conferences for personal or social purposes. With video conferencing, people can feel they must make eye contact with each participant, while also dealing with potential mirror anxiety from seeing their own image on the screen and having a hyperawareness on what they say and do from feeling as though all eyes are on them. This has the potential to lead to too much stimulation and a lot of overthinking.

So, when scheduling virtual meetings, do it with the awareness that these things can be struggles for some people. Make sure there is ample time between video conferences and aim to have other ways to connect and build community as well. Smaller and one-on-one meetings are going to be a better way to build connection than larger group calls. If you mainly have work-related virtual meetings, consider trying a virtual meeting in a social setting by casually reaching out to a colleague about having a virtual coffee or lunch. You can think about starting a virtual book club with your colleagues or a casual group or club related to personal interests. If you can do some of these things in person, even better. If someone is local, set up a time to meet up in person for a walking meeting. Aim to put in calendar reminders for friends' and colleagues' birthdays and important events and reach out to them. I promise people will remember that you cared enough to reach out for important dates in their life. On days that you are feeling isolated, go for a walk, phone or video call a family member, make plans with friends, or visit a local coffee shop where you can see some smiling faces. Ask for help and get support if you are struggling. There are so many ways to build a solid community as a remote or hybrid worker. How can you start deepening those bonds today?

I recently had an onboarding virtual meeting with a speaking bureau and there were four people in the meeting, none of whom I had met in person. We were able to briefly introduce ourselves and get to know one another a bit, and before ending the call there were plans for the next steps and where we needed to go from there. Shortly after, I received an email from a member of the virtual meeting asking if we could set up a time for a quick phone call to get to know one another a bit better. I was impressed. Suggesting that informal call was a wonderful way to add another layer of communication and connection to our partnership. If you are able to talk with someone one on one, that is going to have a different feel, a different vibe, and a different outcome than if you are in a group setting.

Checkpoint

Do you feel like your current team trusts you? Do you trust them? Do you feel connected to the members of your team?

But it's not just checking the box of "communicating." *How* you communicate is crucial to developing healthy working relationships. At the end of the day, we all just want to feel we are heard and understood. This is why developing active listening skills and practicing mindfulness in your conversations is so important. Being present and engaged while someone is talking to you and then paraphrasing what they shared shows them that you were paying attention. By doing so, you are telling them that they matter to you. Using a person's name makes them feel important and seen. Asking questions to learn more about your colleagues' and clients' needs helps them feel understood. Ask them how you can help or support them. There are also some little things that you can do to help people feel at ease. When you are on video calls, try to use welcoming body language. For example, crossing your arms can make you seem closed off. But don't overthink this or stress about it. And never underestimate the power of a simple smile to build trust and connection.

Your relationship with the world

What is your relationship with the world and the greater good? Are you giving back in some way to your immediate community and your wider community? Are you involved in causes that are meaningful to you? Do you feel connected and supported spiritually? When you get involved in groups or causes that are important to you, you end up surrounding yourself with people who share similar passions and interests. Love dogs? Volunteer at a local dog rescue. Want to support the environment? Look into local clubs that give back, or take a local class about composting. There are countless clubs, groups, and volunteer opportunities that you can get involved in where you can build community and give back at the same time.

When I think about the keys for happiness and success, I believe there are three areas where you need to focus your attention to excel. The first is your relationship with yourself. The second is your relationship with others. And the third is your relationship with the world and something greater than you. If you make these things a priority, taking action by making the necessary tweaks and adjustments throughout the different chapters of your work and life, you are heading in the direction of true fulfillment and work/life harmony.

God willing, when you are 100 years old and you look back on your career and your life, how will you want to feel? If I had to guess, you will want to feel that you prioritized the things that mattered most. That you worked towards awakening and achieving your ultimate potential. That you nurtured and valued your relationships along the way. That you worked and lived in alignment with the things that were meaningful to you. That you were kind to yourself and showed yourself love. That you were brave. That you made the moments in your work and life high-quality moments. That you had lots of fun adventures along the way. You will want to feel proud of who you were and of who you are, and the impact you have had on others and on the world. You will want to feel that you worked and lived in harmony with your authentic self. That you accomplished the mission that you, and just you, were meant for.

Endnotes

1   Seppala, E. (2014) *Connectedness & Health: The Science of Social Connection*. http://ccare.stanford.edu/uncategorized/connectedness-health-the-science-of-social-connection-infographic/

2   *Ibid*.

3   Grenny, J. & Maxfield, D. (2017) *A Study of 1,100 Employees Found That Remote Workers Feel Shunned and Left Out*. https://hbr.org/2017/11/a-study-of-1100-employees-found-that-remote-workers-feel-shunned-and-left-out

4   Kraus, M.W.(2017) Voice-only communication enhances empathic accuracy. *American Psychologist*, 72(7): 644–54. https://doi.org/10.1037/amp0000147

5   Queiroz, A.C.M., Lee, A.Y., Luo, M., Fauville, G., Hancock, J.T. & Bailenson, J.N. (2023) Too tired to connect: Understanding the associations between video-conferencing, social connection and well-being through the lens of Zoom fatigue. *Computers in Human Behavior*, 149: 107968. https://doi.org/10.1016/j.chb.2023.107968

6 Fauville, G., Luo, M., Queiroz, A.C.M., Lee, A.Y., Bailenson, J.N. & Hancock, J.T. (2023) Video-conferencing usage dynamics and nonverbal mechanisms exacerbate Zoom Fatigue, particularly for women. *Computers in Human Behavior Reports*, 10: 100271. https://doi.org/10.1016/j.chbr.2023.100271

Acknowledgments

Getting this book to the finish line was 100% a team effort and I am so incredibly grateful to all those in my life who have helped me along the way. An enormous thank you to my husband, Brian who has been by my side every step of the way. Thank you for being an amazing listener, for letting me vent when I need it, for helping me brainstorm ideas, and for always helping me be the best version of myself. You are the most amazing husband, best friend and father to our children. I couldn't have done this without you. A huge thank you to my incredible children who always bring a smile to my face and who inspire me every day. I am so blessed to be your mother. Thank you for being you! To my incredible parents, thank you for your unconditional love and support and for always believing in me. I am so incredibly thankful to be your daughter! To Barb and Tim who are always there to help. Thank you for your positivity, optimism, and your overall amazingness! To my wonderful sisters who always have my back, and to the rest of my incredible, amazing, fun, and loving family, thank you! I am so grateful for all your love and support. A huge thank you to all my friends and to everyone who has supported *Work-Life Tango*. It means more than you know! A gigantic thank you to the publishing team at John Murray Business. I am so grateful to have been able to work with such an amazing group of people. A huge thank you to my editor, Jonathan Shipley, for believing in me and this book. A big thank you to Kaitlyn Shokes for her beautiful work, marketing support and speedy replies and thank you to my literary agent, Linda Konner for helping me navigate being a first-time author. I also want to thank you, the reader. Thank you for reading this. Thank you for making your happiness and well-being a priority. Writing *Work-Life Tango* has been an incredible journey and I am so grateful that you have been a part of it.

Index